Intercultural Performance Studies

OrangeBooks Publication

1st Floor, Rajhans Arcade, Mall Road, Kohka, Bhilai, Chhattisgarh 490020

Website:**www.orangebooks.in**

First Edition, 2024

ISBN: 978-93-5621-542-9

Intercultural Performance Studies

Editors

Dr. Mariana B. M. Andraus
(University of Campinas)

Dr. K. R. Rajaravivarma
(Pondicherry University)

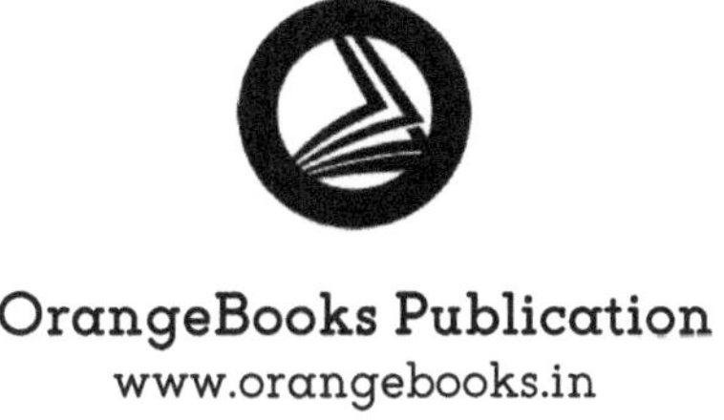

OrangeBooks Publication
www.orangebooks.in

Summary

Authors' Biography

Dr. Sumesh PB

Dr. Sumesh PB is an accomplished actor, director, and Kalarippayattu exponent. He graduated from the School of Drama Thrissur, earned his Post Graduate degree from Hyderabad Central University, and obtained his Ph.D. from Pondicherry University in theatre. Dr. Sumesh served as an artist in the Theatre In Education Company at the National School of Drama for approximately six years. With a rich repertoire, he has acted in numerous plays and directed several productions for children as well as adults. Additionally, he has contributed to the world of cinema by acting in and directing short films as part of Brazil and India Intercultural Performance.

As a distinguished visiting faculty member, Dr. Sumesh has imparted his expertise at esteemed institutions such as the National School of Drama, Jamia Milia Islamia University, Delhi, Sri Ram Centre for Performing Arts, and Samarth Theatre etc. He is renowned for his innovative teaching pedagogy in both actor training and Kalarippayattu. Dr. Sumesh has conducted extensive workshops for children in Theatre in Education and Drama In Education, as well as for teachers at various institutions including The Khaitan School, Noida, Azim Premji University, Bangalore, and Step By Step School, Noida.

Moreover, he has generously shared his skills with Special Needs Children from various NGOs in Delhi. Dr. Sumesh is recognized as a Technical Official of Kalarippayattu games in the National Games 2023 and Khelo India Youth Games 2021, 2022, and 2023. Additionally, he holds a 3rd Dan Black Belt in Karate-do. His contributions to the arts have been acknowledged through prestigious accolades such as the Young Artist Scholarship of the Ministry of Culture and the Junior Research Fellowship of the Ministry of Culture, Government of India. Dr. Sumesh has also made significant scholarly contributions, including the publication of an article on "Kalarippayattile Vaividhyangalum Keralathinte Pothu Samskarika Paramparyavum" in the book 'Kalari Paramparyavum Anuseelanavum', and the presentation of numerous papers in the field of theatre on various topics.

Andrea Itacarambi Albergaria

Andrea Itacarambi Albergaria (Andrea Albergaria) is a PhD student in Performing Arts, at Unicamp, Institute of Arts, Campinas, SP, Brazil, where she develops her research based on the Indian Odissi dance in diaspora, mainly through the production and creation of video scenes and soundscapes. Odissi dance teacher and performer, she is also author of Mudras, the Indian dance gesture as body calligraphy in the contemporary scene (CRV, 2020) and co-author of Traces of Odissi dance: women in teaching, research and performance in Brazil (CRV, 2021) with her advisor Prof. Dr. Mariana Baruco Machado Andraus. Her research is supported by CAPES (Coordenação de Aperfeiçoamento de Pessoal de Nível Superior/ Coordination for the Improvement of Higher Education Personnel).

Aiswarya Lakshmi. G

Aiswarya Lakshmi. G (Aiswarya Lakshmi) is a Bharatanatyam practitioner, teacher and researcher trained from Kalakshetra Foundation, Chennai, India. She has a Masters in Performing Arts from University of Hyderabad, India and is pursuing PhD in Performing Arts under the guidance of Dr. K. R. Rajaravivarma at Department of Performing Arts, Pondicherry University.

Her area of interests are the Narrative and interpretive elements in Bharatanatyam, interrelations among the expressive techniques of classical dances of India, employing yoga, martial arts and drama in dance.

Adriana Suely Queiroz Ribeiro

Adriana Suely Queiroz Ribeiro (Drica Ribeiro), artist from São Paulo of amazonian origin. Master in Performing Arts (dance, theater and performance) from Unicamp. Physical educator specializing in yoga and tai chi pai lin, thai yoga massage therapist and acupuncturist. She combines art, meditation and deep ecology in her work with the body and the ancestral voice. Singer, composer and dancer of poetics of amazonian knowledge practices and teaches asian body arts as well as chanting indian and tibetan mantras. She studies two of the eight forms of indian classical dance, kathak and bharatanatyam and in this field, she has established a fertile intercultural dialogue in the performing arts that relate the study of dance and performance that combine intercultural poetics. She traveled through Brazil, India, Thailand, Portugal, Spain, USA, Finland, Peru, Chile, Argentina and Italy where she received different influences from tribal songs and dances from different parts of the world. These countries was her laboratory to produce sound and body percussion laboratories linked to her indigenous and amazonian ancestral matrices in an intracultural relationship with asian body arts. She traveled throughout Brazil and Europe, performing in different locations, combining songs, dance, body percussion and ancestry in fusions.Drica develops an in-depth study of art activism (ecoperformance) and the ritualistic character of performances in resonance with interculturality. Published a chapter on the body-memory and kathakars, actor-dancers, in the book "Intercultural Studies in Presencial Arts" (published by CRV). In 2022 she published, with a collective of artists, the book of poetry "Body, animal em extinction" (publisher Urutau) about amazonian poetics. Drica has a degree in Thai Yoga Massage in Brazil and also in Tailand since 2012 and teaches classes, workshops, courses and lectures in schools, therapeutic spaces, colleges and universities about the benefits of the body culture of peace and the importance of reconnecting with oneself and with the wisdom of the body. Her work is focused on self-knowledge and meditation combined with the ecology of knowledge as natural ways of cultivating a healthy body, mind and spirit. She works in training actors, dancers and stage artists, seeking to establish a constant dialogue between dance and performance with asian body techniques. She believes in the union between science and spirituality as effective means to help artists improve themselves, cultivate their internal balance, creativity and expand their inner potential.

Cassiana Rodrigues Santana

Cassiana Rodrigues Santana (Cassiana Rodrigues) has a Bachelor's degree in Performing Arts from the Federal University of the State of Rio de Janeiro, a Degree in Visual Arts from the Claretiano University Center, a Master's degree in Performing Arts from the State University of Campinas, where she is also a doctoral student. Since 2000, she has continuously dedicated herself to studying forms of dance-theater through research focused on the body and its ways of expression, with the Mohiniyattam and Kuchipudi dance styles as some of its pillars. For more than ten years, she has been investigating the relationships between Indian dance and the religious manifestations of Afro-Brazilian culture through movement and gestural codes. She works as an actress, dancer, teacher, choreographer and researcher.

Jonatas Lopes de Matos Santos

Jonatas Lopes de Matos Santos (Jonatas Matos) is a dance artist, martial artist, and art educator. He researches the relationships between symbolic and movement repertoires of martial arts and dance, in dialogue with Afro-

Diasporic and East Asian perspectives. He is a master's and undergraduate student in Dance at the School of Dance at the Federal University of Bahia (UFBA), a specialist in Art Education from the School of Fine Arts at UFBA, and holds a degree in Social Communication: Communication and Culture Production.

Milena Pereira dos Santos

Milena Pereira dos Santos (Milena Pereira) is a circus and dance artist. Currently, she is a doctoral student, through a cotutelle arrangement, in the Humanities Program at Concordia University and the Performing Arts Program of the University of Campinas, Brazil.

Flávia Pagliusi

Flávia Pagliusi is a Brazilian psychoanalyst, dance researcher and director. She is a PhD student at Unicamp and has a Master degree in Performing Arts at the same University. Death, grief and the intertwining between psyche and body are subjects of her investigation.

Mariana B. M. Andraus

Dr. Mariana Baruco Machado Andraus (Mariana Baruco) is a dancer, choreographer, martial artist and dance researcher. She is Associate Professor at the Department of Performing Arts of the University of Campinas (Unicamp, Brazil). She works with contemporary dance and creative processes related to Western and Eastern dance techniques. She is author/organiser of 12 books, 18 chapters and 30 papers about diversified issues in Performing Arts area. She shares with Professor Dr. K.R. Rajaravivarma the coordination of Intercultural Studies in Performing Arts research group.

Introduction

Dr. K. R. Rajaravivarma
Dr. Mariana B. M. Andraus

It is an effort put forward together by the Department of Performing Arts of the University of Campinas, Brazil, and the Pondicherry University, India, to create twenty-nine pieces of Intercultural performances during the covid-19 pandemic as well as subsequently after the pandemic. The history of Performing Arts always demands time to time practical attempts and theoretical discussions for the development or evolution of the field. Sometimes performances led to discussion and vice-versa. It was a successful journey from 2019 to 2022 amongst the members of the research forum which contained scholars and faculties of both universities and the integration of individual performing arts practitioners who joined together having the objectives of creating performances out of their art forms and experiential practices in the online *modus operandi*.

In 2019, Prof. Mariana Baruco Machado Andraus, coordinator of the Postgraduate Programs of the Institute of Arts, at University of Campinas (UNICAMP), introduced Irani da Cruz Cippiciani, a Ph.D. research scholar, to me through an internship program on Therukuthu research for the period of three months from December 2018 to March 2019. Irani's prior association with the Koothu-P-Pattarai, Chennai, Theatre group and its artistic director N.Muthuswamy's guidance in the background of her research on Therukuthu made a compelling case to offer her the internship program under my guidance at the Department of Performing Arts, Pondicherry University.

Earlier in my life, I was a full-time actor, actor trainer and rehearsal director at Koothu-P-Pattarai and traversed through the industry for thirteen years (1992 – 2004). During her interaction and interview with me, she found the importance of the Therukuthu form in the training system of performers and its relevance to contemporary performances and play productions of the Tamils in Tamilnadu and Puducherry.

Further, she interviewed an anthropologist and Therukuthu field expert Dr.A.Chellaperumal, Professor and Head of the Department of Anthropology, Pondicherry University. He shared with her some vital information and research paper materials on the art form of Theukuthu and the folk theatre of Tamilnadu. Soon after the event of successful completion and submission of her PhD thesis under the guidance of Prof. Dr Cassiano Sydow Quilici at the University of Campinas, Brazil, Irani looked forward to further interactions with us.

With all these past fruitful experiences with Pondicherry University, Irani invited Prof. A. Chellaperumal and me to induct as members of the Research forum for the discussion and to intercommunicate between the Department of Performing Arts, University of Campinas, and the Department of Performing Arts, Pondicherry University. It was initiated and led by Prof. Mariana and her scholars. In the first meeting, our objectives were to find various possibilities on "How to intercommunicate the thoughts on the individual research that the scholars selected and the specialized area of research. We also discussed different possibilities to commence those ideologies". As we progressed this ideology through a few meetings, we found out that simply vocally communicating the ideologies through the committee was limited to our intention. Then we shifted our area of interest towards intercultural performance and online performances. We called it "The Research Forum for Intercultural Performances

Studies".

The first performance was an enticing and inspirational output from our department where instructor Dr P.Murugavel's music was adapted well within the piece of the work " Books, Flowers and the Pestilence" done by Cassiana and Rafael, under the concept, editing and designed by Prof. Mariana. Soon after we realized the succession of the performance that commemorated the envisionment of our collaboration. We invited new proposals from scholars and faculty members on both sides in Brazil and India for the individual explorations of the participants with a duration of one to five minutes.

The process of interjecting music, editing, interpretation, etc., was done with dedication and a long vision after collecting feedback from both sides through several one-line meetings with Prof. Mariana and her team. I found that those twenty-nine experimental performances were done with an enormous effort from every individual artist – scholar during and after the covid-19 pandemic. This made me realize that the art and culture would never die even if artists are conditioned to live in any isolated space and time in any parts of the world. The proliferation and advancements in the mass communication technologies have enabled artists to share their performances and ideologies across the global audience.

We feel that it is the pivotal initiation towards future collaborative works between the departments of the respective Universities and especially this book of writing from the participants of research scholars on their experimental performances. It will remain a historical mark in this field of intercultural performance studies for global reference. In the next phase, we expect the direct interaction of scholars and faculties through exchange programs, fieldwork, cultural tours, workshops, and joined inter-cultural performance-making projects in Brazil and India through MoU.

Dr.K.R.RAJARAVIVARMA,

Associate Professor,

Department of Performing Arts,

Pondicherry University,

Kalapet, Puducherry - 65014.

Ph.9444713034/7418793034

Email: avkoodam@pondiuni.ac.in /

avkoodam@live.com

About the proposal, by Mariana B. M. Andraus

I have been a professor at the Postgraduate Program in Performing Arts at the University of Campinas (Unicamp), Brazil, since 2013. I was coordinator of this postgraduate program between 2015 and 2017 and, in this position, I had direct contact with the research of all program students. One of them, Irani Cippiciani, benefited from a FAPESP scholarship and, through this scholarship, she carried out a Sandwich Doctorate at Pondicherry University, in India, under the guidance of professor Dr. K. R. Rajaravivarma, and this was the first contact I had with him.

I have always been interested in Indian dance, which I studied informally and with some interruptions, always in Brazil and with Brazilian teachers, since 2012. I was never an expert on Indian dances. I like the Odissi technical training (*Chouks, Tribhangs*) and I have learned only three choreographies so far *(Mangalacharan, Vasant Pallavi* and *Srita Kamala*). I practice them simply because these practices calm me down and I enjoy them, and I can really connect with the music more than most western styles. During the pandemic, it ended up becoming a kind of healing ritual, since we couldn't go out to train at the University, and these choreographies can be trained in a relatively small space. So, I trained them in my living room as a diary ritual all along 2020-2022.

Between 2019 and 2020, already as Associate Director of the Institute of Arts at Unicamp, I started working on establishing a flow for approval of research groups at the institute. In my trajectory, research and administrative work have always been mixed. So, after creating the flow that would serve all researchers, I felt it was time to open my own research group at Unicamp.

I had a research trajectory strongly linked to Chinese Martial Arts, which were my research topic in my master's and doctorate research; a strong interest in Indian dances, and a history linked to research in Brazilian dances, especially the Afro-diasporic ones, which are the special brand of the curriculum at Unicamp. Furthermore, I was guided in the doctorate by Professor Dr. Inaicyra Falcão dos Santos, a specialist in Nagô-Yorubá traditions, and with her I had the opportunity of reflections and very rich exchanges involving the traditions of Candomblé and Umbanda *terreiros[1]*, which are the two most popular Afro-Brazilian religions, full of very enchanting dance and music references.

I am an Umbanda[2] practitioner, and I was practically born in a *terreiro*. For me, the dimension of the sacred is and has always been very important, and I have always been strongly impacted by the archetypal strength of the figures of the Orixás[3]. On the other hand, precisely for this reason, I have always been extremely zealous in not letting these two sectors of my life, professional dance, and religion, mix to each other, precisely to preserve my sacredness. In 2023, to my enormous surprise, I was nominated to become the leader of the *terreiro* I grew up in, and a new cycle begins in my life precisely at the very moment I write this text.

This trajectory outside the university ends up helping me to guide research also in the field of Afro-diasporic dances, since I know them from this mentioned personal experience. Although my *terreiro*, specifically, does not have dances as part of the ritual, I know them from knowing other *terreiros*. So, to create a research group that would encompass all the research that I supervise at Unicamp, I thought of tracing the discussion

---

1 *Terreiro* is the place where Umbanda and Candomblé rituals happen.

2 Umbanda is a religion born from the syncretism between the different people that make up the Brazilian identity.

3 Orixás are deities originating from the Nagô-Yoruba traditions, that is, African deities, which in Umbanda are transformed and come to be conceptualized as leaders of spiritual "lines" with which disembodied spirits, especially of Indigenous and Africans, but not only, are attuned.

on interculturality as its focus and scope, giving rise to discussions that are especially careful to avoid cultural appropriations, focusing, methodologically, in emphasizing listening to the other culture artists and recognizing identifications that go beyond stereotypes.

The pandemic has led artists around the world to discover meeting platforms that make online meetings possible. So, I plucked up courage and sent an email to Professor Dr. K. R. Rajaravivarma, inviting him to a meeting to see if we could try a research partnership. The Professor was extremely receptive and, since then, he has always been very open to proposals for artistic action that I send to the group, which in general are not so orthodox.

In Brazil we are always encouraged to break with traditions and create dances in unusual ways. However, I gradually realized that the "responses" we prepared for the letters (in general, more "contemporary") were not so contrasting with the responses sent by the Pondicherry researchers. Some videos sent by researchers Sumesh and Aiswarya completely broke with the ideas about Indian dances that I had (see Letters 16 e 23, for example). Certainly, the responses sent by Pondicherry researchers were also enriched by the eclectic formative experience of these artists, which also includes theater and martial arts, among others.

The creation of the videos became a space for experimentation and dialogue between traditions and ruptures, between Indian elements and Brazilian elements, between more serious proposals and more playful ones, and we still tried to learn to explore technology more and more (the more iconic example of this would be Letter 29).

But after all, what is it that we call "Letters"? From triggering texts, all artists recorded videos in response and sent it to the "scenic provocateur", who saw all the materials and mixed them according to his own *criteria*. In this way, the work pairs were formed blindly. An artist didn't create his video to be edited with another artist of his choice; it was the editor, after seeing all the videos, who put the pairs together, depending on what they had answered.

A similar methodology I used in another project, called *Jardim das Cartas*, which I developed with Professor Dr. Jonatas Manzolli, from the Department of Music at Unicamp, but in this other project the mixes were made by software. In the present research, on the contrary, we prioritized the handmaid and human action of an artist analyzing all the materials, choosing and mixing them according to the impressions that each of the video responses caused to him.

In this process, from seven provocations (two launched by me, one by Prof. K. R. Rajaravivarma, one by Paula Ibañez, one by Andrea Albergaria, one by Aiswarya Lakshmi, G. and one by Sumesh P.B.), have been created so far 29 videos, available on this channel:

https://www.youtube.com/@estudosinterculturais6034/videos

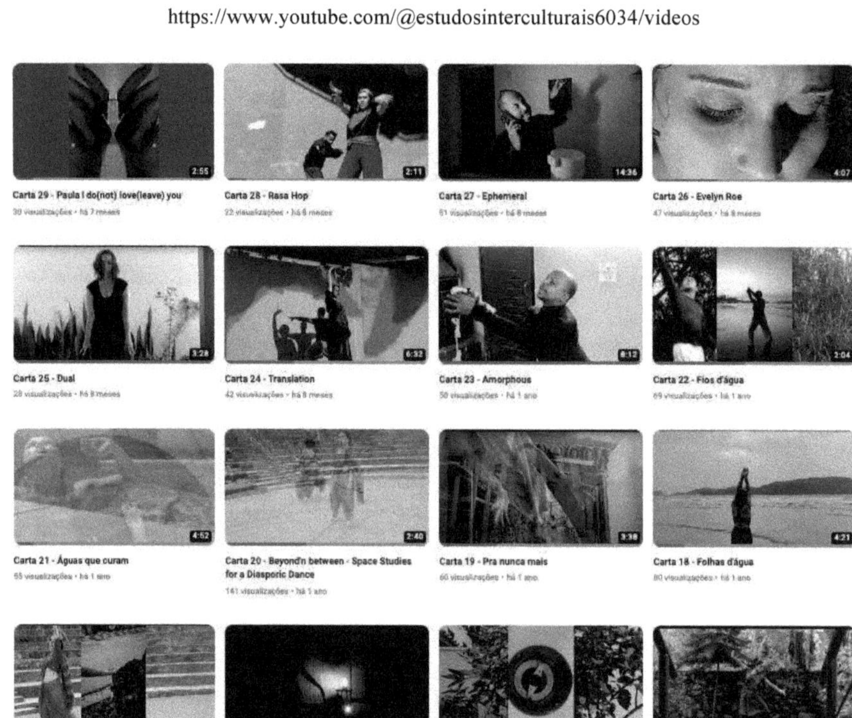

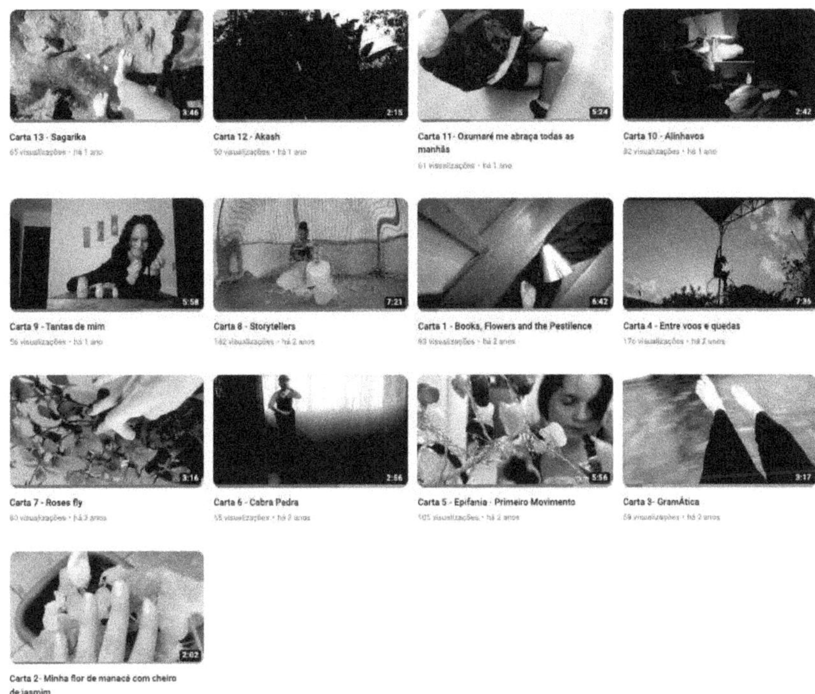

Figure 1. Screenshot of the main page of our YouTube's channel.

The titles of the videos are:

Letter 1- Books, Flowers, and the Pestilence

Letter 2- My manacá flower with jasmine scent

Letter 3- GrammAr

Letter 4- Between Flights and Falls

Letter 5- Epiphany - First Movement

Letter 6- Goat Stone

Letter 7- Roses fly

Letter 8- Storytellers

Letter 9- So Many of Me

Letter 10- Sewing

Letter 11- Oxumaré hugs me every morning

Letter 12- Akash

Letter 13- Sagarika

Letter 14- Maya

Letter 15- Powder Cloud

Letter 16- Light in Shadows

Letter 20- Beyond's between - Space Studies

Letter 21- Healing Waters

Letter 22- Trickles of Water

Letter 23- Amorphous

Letter 24- Translation

Letter 25- Dual

Letter 26- Evelyn Roe

Letter 27- Ephemeral

Letter 28- Rasa Hop

Letter 17- Quiet

Letter 18- Water Leaf

Letter 19- For never more

Letter 29- I do(not) love(leave) you

We invite readers to first watch the videos and then read the chapters. Each artist wrote a chapter commenting on all the videos they participated in, as well as others' videos, analyzing and reflecting on the experience.

With the maturity of the process, after these almost three years of partnership in research and artistic creation, we are now moving towards the formalization of a cooperation agreement between the universities, establishing the research group Intercultural Performance Studies (IPS).

Dr.Mariana Baruco Machado Andraus,

Associate Professor,

Department of Performing Arts,

University of Campinas,

R. Pitagoras, 500, CEP: 13083-854

Ph. 55 19 3521-2437

Email: mandraus@unicamp.br

1

In Search Of Art In Challenging Times (Letters 23 & 27)

Sumesh P.B.[4]

The crust

The history of humanity is also the history of diseases and the development of various mechanisms to control them (Dobson & Carper, 1996). The expansion of cities, the rise of trade crossing seas and continents, increased travel, and the impact of increased population on the environment led to the emergence and spread of infectious diseases, epidemics, and pandemics (Lindahl & Grace, 2015). They exposed the mortality and vulnerability of mankind as well as endangered its very existence. But, on the other side, such pandemics became a determinative juncture in history as they steered crucial and decisive shifts in the way humans get along and connect to one another (Venkatesan, Chatterjee, Lewis, & Callender, 2022). They presented moments to attain new understandings of the human physique and its diverse operations. Simultaneously, it also reflected and reconstructed the ways in which societies and communities formed and connected with each other.

As every pandemic has a social, political, and economic base, such incidents will affect the entire fabric of the concerned society in a transformative manner. The COVID-19 pandemic marked a metamorphosis in the history of mankind as it affected and changed the nature, structure, and course of everything in the social, cultural, political and economic relations of mankind. While it affected the lives of millions of people in every sector, it also paved the way for endless experiments and explorations in all walks of life. Similarly, the pandemic has had an enormous impact on art and literature. While it affected the day-to-day lives of an endless number of artists, it also affected the way in which they

---

4 Ph.D Scholar, Pondicherry University.

expressed themselves. The lockdowns in all societies throughout the world presented new and challenging realities to everyone, particularly those engaged in the cultural front.

The Mantle

The COVID-19 pandemic was not the first infectious disease that affected the ordinary lives of people everywhere. Diseases like plague, cholera, flu, SARS and MERS have affected humanity in the past. All of them made major turning points during their associated societies too. The Plague of Justinian was the first pandemic in recorded history. Between 541 AD and 543 AD, it killed around hundred million people in the Roman Empire. The establishment of the Marian festival and the development of iconolatry culture, along with the reconstruction of the image of the emperor as a 'pious saint' were the aftereffects of this outbreak (Meier, 2020). The Black Death of the fourteenth century eliminated around one-third of the European population. It influenced culture by increasing the representation of symbols representing death. The desperation and sadness created by the Black Death were embodied in large numbers of cultural and artistic forms (Kahla, 2019). The enforcement of realism in art is the most significant outcome of the same. The origin of the Dance of Death can be traced to the same circumstances (Cohen, 1982).

Cholera as a pandemic was reported seven times in the 19th and 20th centuries. It affected urban centres and paralysed those societies for decades. Similarly, influenza also altered associated communities. The Russian flu (1889–1893), Spanish flu (1918–1919), and Asian flu (1957–1959) affected certain geographical areas only, whereas the one in 1968–1970 affected three continents (North America, Europe and Asia). The H1N1 pandemic of 2009 also affected several communities in the west.

The emergence of a pandemic challenges and deconstructs the existing nature and structure of cultural formats and society. Such catastrophes were represented in various formats in art, literature and other cultural forms. Among others, their representation is most visible in literary formats. Apart from a large number of academic investigations, these pandemics were narrated fictionally in several novels. Black death becomes the canvas for 'Dooms Day Book' (Connie Willis in 1992) and 'The Decameron Stories' (Giovanni Boccaccio). 'A Journal of the Plague Year' (Daniel Defoe in 1772) and 'Year of Wonders' (Geraldine Brooks in 2001) narrate the impact of the plague on London in 1665. Albert Camus' 'The Plague' (1947) is also about the plague. Igor Stravinsky's 'The Firebird Suite' (1919), Sergei Prokofiev's 'The Love for Three Oranges' (1918), Katherine Ann Porter's 'Pale Horse, Pale Rider' (1939) and William Maxwell's 'They Came Like Swallows' (1937) were about the 1918 influenza pandemic. Tony Kushner's 'Angels in America' (1991) and Randy Shilts' 'And the Band Played on' (1987) were about HIV/AIDS. Similar attempts were made in paintings as well. Edvard Munch's two 'Self-Portraits after the Spanish Flu' (1919), Pieter Bruegel the Elder's 'The Triumph of Death' (1562-63) and Poussin's 'The Plague of Ashdod' (1630–31) are about influenza and plague, respectively. 'Philadelphia' (1993) and 'Dallas Buyers Club (2013) were the cinematic presentations on AIDS.

The cultural reflections or representations are not only the artistic interpretations of them; they also symbolise the vision and enthusiasm of mankind to survive any destructive or disastrous circumstance that arises. They are conscious, intellectual, and sometimes experimental efforts to expose the limitations of existing systems or facilities (Vrdoljak & Bauer, 2020). The multifarious artistic treatments of such impasse from diverse cultures will enrich the multiplicity of observations, understandings, and reactions on the same. Hence, they facilitate realising the intensity and breadth of the impact of such events in ordinary language, excluding jargon. Consequently, such records function to metamorphically transform the existing society to face pandemics later.

The responses from art and literature also represent indigenous knowledge as well as notions about pandemics. They reflect on the formation and sharing of pandemic knowledge at the bottom level. The local interpretations of social, economic, and political causes and consequences of such outbreaks aid in the improvement of common understanding, which makes them prepared, consciously, or otherwise, for another pandemic. Compared to medical and scientific measures, these cultural artifacts are genuine and original documentation about the willingness and capability of mankind to go through such experiences. In other words, they make and reflect on the impactful knowledge of communities.

Compared to all earlier pandemics or epidemics, Corona in 2020 presented a unique picture in its reach and impacts. When all previous ones affected a large geographical area, Corona affected almost everyone on the globe. The high spreading rate of the disease led to serious and urgent precautionary measures from all communities and governments everywhere. This resulted in worldwide lockdown as well as social distancing in all societies. The absence of mass gatherings adversely affected the entire theatre and performing arts sector in all countries.

The venues of such activities were either closed or reduced their audience capacities to prevent the spread of the pandemic, which resulted in a significant reduction in live performance.

So, theatre companies and performing teams faced significant financial losses. Even those shows permitted were not financially viable as they had only a limited number of viewers due to social distancing. When some of them shifted to virtual platforms, they presented new challenges for performers and production teams. The travel restrictions led to the loss of jobs or a reduction in income for many performers and production staff. This adversely affected the morale and confidence of theatre artists worldwide. Even those live performances on virtual platforms presented uncertainty for many performers due to connectivity issues and a lack of expertise. This led to insecurity and anxiety among many theatre artists, particularly among younger ones.

The shift to virtual performances has also presented new challenges for theatre artists, who must adapt their craft to a new medium and learn new skills such as filming and editing. This has led to a sense of disconnection from the live performance experience, which can be a source of inspiration and motivation for many theatre artists. Hence, most of them felt uncertain about the future of their careers and the future of the theatre industry. However, there are also many examples of resilience, creativity, and innovation within the theatre community, with artists finding new ways to connect with audiences and create meaningful work despite the challenges.

The Core

When lockdown presented a standstill in theatre performances, Intercultural Studies in Performing Arts paved the way for a new experiment to many of us. The invitation to develop a solo performance and to record it for sharing among a wider community of like-minded artists across continents is innovative as well as inspiring. More than that, the attempt to positively respond to the invitation transformed the limited space of the home into a performing altar. That enabled us to discover new valleys of possibility within the least available and shrinking space here. As a result, two amateur plays with the titles 'Amorphous' and 'Ephemeral' were made and recorded.

The Amorphous reflects the true shape and identity of human life through the medium of water which is the abstract symbol of life. The tagline of the play itself is "Water is body and body is water". As amorphous literally means "without a clearly defined shape or form", water does not have an identity of its own. It incorporates the shape, color, taste or smell of what it deals with. The identity-less character of water is reflected in the purest form of humanity, i.e., the new-born baby. A baby is formed within the chemical or biological water inside the womb of the mother. At the end of life, the body disintegrates into soil as water (body fluids). In between, around sixty percent of the human body itself is water. Apart from that, water is present throughout the life of a man. His social, economic, and political relationships are either directly or indirectly connected to water. This play tries to reflect on that.

In the opening scene, one person is shown struggling with tissue paper. The man wrapped in white tissue paper symbolises the soul struggling to come out of nature. Later, the soul becomes free as it is born. He sees, smells, tastes, and experiences life as a response to the realities around him. His life becomes meaningful only in the presence of those around him. That experience was beautiful, like a flower. The flower he carries in the play reflects it. The puppet made from yarn symbolises the cute but very fragile physical body. And finally, the end of life also happens. Death is inevitable. The rituals were conducted as expected. The lifeless body in the form of a puppet is set on fire. The remaining ashes at the end are collected in a mud pot. As part of the rituals, the pot is opened later to wash out the ashes in water. The ashes merge with the water. What is created in water finally ends up there alone.

The eternal meaning of life lies in its mortality. Like water, it is very simple in essence. But in response to whatever happens around us, we assume unneeded interpretations of the value of life. We adapt the color, taste, smell and finally the shape of something around us and become impure in the process of living. The reality is exposed only at the end. All those exhibitions in life become irrelevant then.

Ephemeral is another play that portraits the identity crisis of humans. The play shows only a few hours in the life of a modern man. His life is very mechanical or routine-like. He goes to work in the morning and returns in the evening. In between, he adopts many identities. In each situation, he behaves and interacts with people accordingly. That means he continuously and consistently adapts to situations and, in the process, adopts distinct identities. Thus, he does not have an identity of his own, or his identity is one of adapting different identities from time to time. This is an identity crisis.

The character in the play is very neutral in the beginning. But as time passes, the speed of his actions gradually rises. He receives phone calls from time to time. According to each call, his body language and rhythm are also changing. Finally, he comes to his own room. There he is relaxing and becoming happy. As is understandable from the above, the phone is also becoming a crucial character in the play. Its presence is felt throughout. The identity crisis is, in a way, the creation of phone calls made by different people. He responds to different people differently. But in the process of talking to different people vividly, he gets irritated and finally becomes abnormal. The transformation of the phone into a knife and stabbing it in the ear shows the irritation created by the identity crisis itself. But in that way, he loses the phone and becomes cool.

The play shows both the bright and dark shades of life. The increasing pace of modern life and its technological gadgets only complicate things. Everyone is going through this. Hence, all are facing some degree of identity crisis. The nature of modern life demands diverse kinds of responses from individuals, which makes them vulnerable too. It is striking to note that the lighting in the play is very central to its theme. The 'shadows' symbolise the hollowness of the hectic life schedule we all follow. Shadows accompany everything, everywhere. That is the essence of life. Life moves through issues and struggles to address them. It is cyclical in nature.

Now it is important to review whether the format and content of plays overwhelm the challenges presented by the corona pandemic. Considering the lockdown, making of solo performances, and sharing them on virtual platforms is the most feasible mechanism to keep the spirit of theatre. Even though pose some challenges to old people, the available digital technologies in the phone help to record and edit such videos. Considering the lack of live venues, it is the only option to do theatre. Regarding the content, both plays were doing justice to the need of time. As pandemic created a fear of death to everyone, the Amorphous reflects the futility of life itself. Even though humans claims that they achieved everything they wished, in reality we all were adapting the 'shapes' decided by the circumstances, like water assuming the shape of where it contain. The misunderstanding of men about their achievements led to highly paced routine life where identity crisis repeatedly occurs. The same is the theme of 'Ephemeral'.

Conclusion

However, the real impacts of a metamorphosis pandemic like COVID-19 will be more cultural and social than economic. The sectors that rely on physical locations (such as galleries, theatres, live performances, festivals, etc.) are those that are most negatively impacted by social distancing policies. But the artists attempted to innovate through digitalization. This enabled a new network of artists and performers who reside in different countries or continents. Along with that, it also helped to discover new themes and talents in society. Hence, all these efforts raise the hope that humanity can overcome any threat by innovating itself.

References

Cohen, J. (1982). Death and the Danse Macabre. *History Today*, 32 (8), 35-40.

Dobson, A. P., Carper, E. R. (1996). Infectious Diseases and Human Population History: throughout History the Establishment of Disease has been a Side Effect of the Growth of Civilization. *BioScience, 46*(2), 115-126.

Kahla, M. (2019). Arrows of Affliction: The Bubonic Plague and Its Representation in Medieval Art and Literature. *The Saber and Scroll Journal, 8*(1), 29-47.

Lindahl, J. F., Grace, D. (2015). The Consequences of Human Actions on Risks for Infectious Diseases: A Review. *Infection Ecology and Epidemiology*, 5.

Meier, M. (2020). The 'Justinianic Plague': An Inconsequential Pandemic? A Reply.

Medizinhistorisches, 55(2), 172-199.

Venkatesan, S., Chatterjee, A., Lewis, A. D., Callender, B. (2022). Introduction. In S.

Venkatesan, A. Chatterjee, A. D. Lewis, B. *Callender, Pandemics and Epidemics in Cultural Representation* (pp. 1-10). Singapore: Springer.

Vrdoljak, A. F., Bauer, A. A. (2020). Pandemics and the Role of Culture. *International Journal of Cultural Property, 27*(4), 441-448

2

"Letter 27 – Ephemeral": A Battle Of Shadows And Swords

Andrea Itacarambi Albergaria

Inspired by two works that emerged during our pandemic and intercultural exchanges, I bring here some personal observations about the video "Carta 27 - Ephemeral", created by Sumesh PB from the proposal "dual, or two sides of a coin", sent by Aishwarya Lakshmi. Both artists are PhD students at the Department of Performing Arts, University of Pondicherry, and supervised by Prof. Raja Ravivarma, whom I had the honor of meeting in person. I look for support in Schechner's performance studies (2013), psychological states from Jung (2008), anthropological theatre from Barba (1991) (all of them have been in India for research), and my own experience as an Odissi dancer. Directing my observation in relation to the result of the work "Carta 27 - Ephemeral" as part of our Intercultural Performing Arts group, coordinated also by Prof. Dra. Mariana Baruco, from Arts Institute, Unicamp, Brazil, I´m going first towards to interculturality concept that, according to Schechner's (2013) words, means:

Intercultural: between or among two or more cultures (rather than nations). Intercultural performances emphasize what connects or is shared or what separates or is unique; an intercultural performance may be harmonic or dissonant; or both (SCHECHNER, 2013, p. 263).

And still according to him, intercultural performances occur not only between different cultures, but also at the interfaces of technologies, where presence occurs through interactions and incursions into spaces other than the stage, the rehearsal room or any other physical place.

In terms of performance studies, the "intercultural question" involves valuing embodied and digital as well as written and archived knowledge. (...) Intercultural performances both digitally and in person; scholarship too is conducted face-to-face and by means of internet conferencing.

Digital knowledge and experience is not a settled category. From one perspective, it appears archival; from another, very "live". Chatrooms, streaming video, instant messaging, picture messaging, face-to-face or video phone calls, live telecasting, podcasting, social media, blogs, and the like create expanding, dynamic spaces that are not face-to-face and not face to-face; spaces between "present," "ongoing," and "finished" (SCHECHNER, 2013, p. 328).

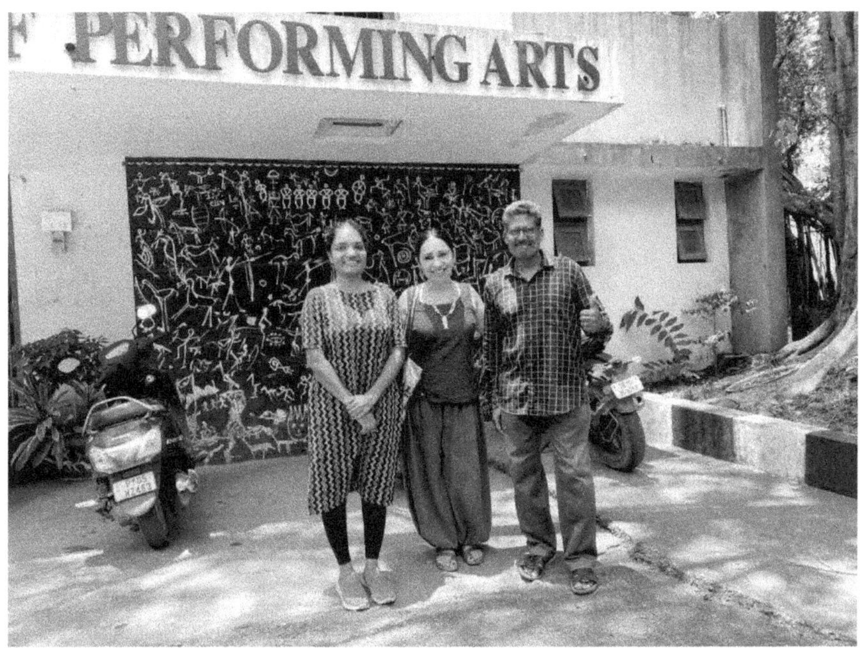

Figure 1. Meeting with Prof. RajaRaviVarma, Head of the Department of Performing Arts at the University of Pondicherry and Aishwarya Lakshmi, Phd student. *Source:* Personal Archive. Picture by Lucia Minozzo, 2023.

The proposal received was open to any reading option, and each one of us brought his creation. Sumesh's "Carta 27 - Ephemeral" work brought to light the daily life of a man pressed by multiplicity of communication. In an exhausting cycle of variations in his emotional states, this man is eternally connected by technology to countless calls from his cell phones. But at the same time, in that place he got some moments of relax and fun. Through this context, emotions were rapidly transformed according to phone received calls: changes in emotional states were rapid, transient states between coming to and going to work through telephone conversations. This videoscene portrays the life of contemporary man, where simultaneous communications permeate the 24 hours of the day, causing all kinds of stress, for an eternal condition of being available. In the video, the walks to and from work become a frame for the cauldron of sensations that will unfold. "Carta 27 - Ephemeral" is a complaint, a protest to the pressure suffered by the number of communications through the technologies of the present. At the same time, it is through them that we author and performer, brings the atmosphere of the abstract connected and can, as artists, take our work to non-face-to-face audiences, unknown audiences, in the borderless place that is the globalized world.

In cosmopolitan urban areas, avant-garde and experimental performance and performance art react against globalization even as they participate in it. Artists savaging the global system are only too happy to tour globally to deliver their message far and wide (SCHECHNER, 2013, p. 321).

"Carta 27 - Ephemeral" provokes a certain mirroring, psychological behavior that shows, at some point, we can identify with this work: we see ourselves in similar situations when emotions come out fighting through our own shadows. By the way, shadows and light are used in the psychological field by another psychologist, who had been in India in the past century, and transformed his own work into a kind of interculturality. For Carl Jung (2008, p.174), shadows concepts are largely identified when they are shown as their light also: "(...) It is a psychological rule that the brighter the light, the blacker the shadow; in other words, the more rationalistic we are in our conscious minds, the more alive becomes the spectral world of the unconscious."

In these altered states of mind, "Carta 27 - Ephemeral" alludes to the two cell phones with two bladed weapons, two knives, which, in addition to fighting each other, also fight with the actor's shadow projected on the wall. Entering the universe of ephemera and abstractions, this work reminded me of a scene of Butoh, while creating opposition worlds at the same time joining them. On Schechner´s studies:

[...] butoh: literally, "stamping dance." The first butoh performance was Kinjiki (1959) choreographed by Hijikata Tatsumi who, along with Ohno Kazuo founded butoh. Hijikata called his dancing ankoku butoh or "dark dance." The dark side of butoh is based on a nonrational collision of images and sounds. After Hijikata and Ohno, many individuals and groups, both Japanese and non-Japanese, have performed butoh. Butoh's intense performance style and underlying philosophy draw on Japanese martial arts and classical dance, German expressionist dance, Shinto, shamanism, and Zen. At present, butoh is both very Japanese and part of the global culture of experimental performance (SCHECHNER, 2013, p. 310).

As an actor trained into the Indian martial art Kalaripayattu. Sumesh PB, "Carta 27 - Ephemeral"'s author and performer, brings the atmosphere of the abstract into reality. Kalaripayattu also crossed the boundaries, and still, it is an Indian art, also belongs to global culture nowadays, as a technique not only for fighting, but for artists looking for tools to build corporeality, tonus, focus and concentration. Kalaripayattu, Odissi, Kathakali, Bharat Natyam and many other Indian arts expressions were larged studied by Italian dramaturg Eugenio Barba (1991), following steps of his theatrical searches partner Jerzy Grotowski (1933-1999), who started this research on India artistic ancestral techniques for drama acting in 60's. Using the concept of pre-expressiveness as an important element for scenic construction, this term coined by Eugenio Barba (1991, p. 197) has its source on Asian arts and is present in his work "A Dictionary of Theatre Anthropology". Schechner (2013) discusses the term using Barba's own words:

Pre-expressivity: Widely known and practiced throughout Asia, martial arts use concrete physiological processes to destroy the automatisms of daily life and to create another quality of energy in the body. It is this very aspect of martial arts, that is, their use of acculturation technique, which has inspired codified theatre forms. The legs slightly bent, the arms contracted: the basic position of all Asiatic martial arts shows a decided body ready to leap and to act. This attitude, which could be compared to the plié in classical ballet, can be found in the basic positions of both Oriental and Occidental performers. It is nothing more than a codification, in the form of extra-daily technique, of the position of an animal ready to attack or defend itself (BARBA apud SCHECHNER, 2013, p. 226).

Besides these observations, my look also went to expressions of emotions shown on "Carta 27 - Ephemeral ". These expressions or emotions are common for all cultures around the world, but there's an ancient Indian treatise about them. They are described in Natya Shastra, of Bharat Muni (circa century II BCE - II CE) and presented in a very complex way, with subdivisions and additions. The *rasa* concept or the aesthetic flavor is present in Indian drama and dance theory, and is spread around the globe. Bharat Muni describes eight as main emotions, or *sthai bhava*, and many others can be considered as conductors to some of these eight. As Odissi dance practitioner, I've learnt these main *rasas* named as erotic (*srngara*), comic *(hasya)*, tragic (*karuna*), furious (*raudra*), heroic (*vira*), timorous (*bhayanka*), disgusting (*bibhatsa*), and wondrous (*adbhuta*) doing exercises of eyes, face expression and use body composition. During an *abhinaya*, for example, we must know the main *bhava* in a dramaturgic context to be used for creating *rasa*. Between these two *bhava* and *rasa*, there's a journey of elements conductors (small emotions or instigators), consequential elements and complementary psychological states. During the observation of "Carta 27 - Ephemeral" I could identify some transient emotional states due to the actor's very well-done expressions. From the beginning of work up to the end many different elements had appeared, including contradictory states of mind, different emotions and external elements. From initial *bhava jugupsa* (disgust) we could feel *rasa bibhatsa* (disgusted) at the end, but during the way many emotions or fragmented feelings came out.

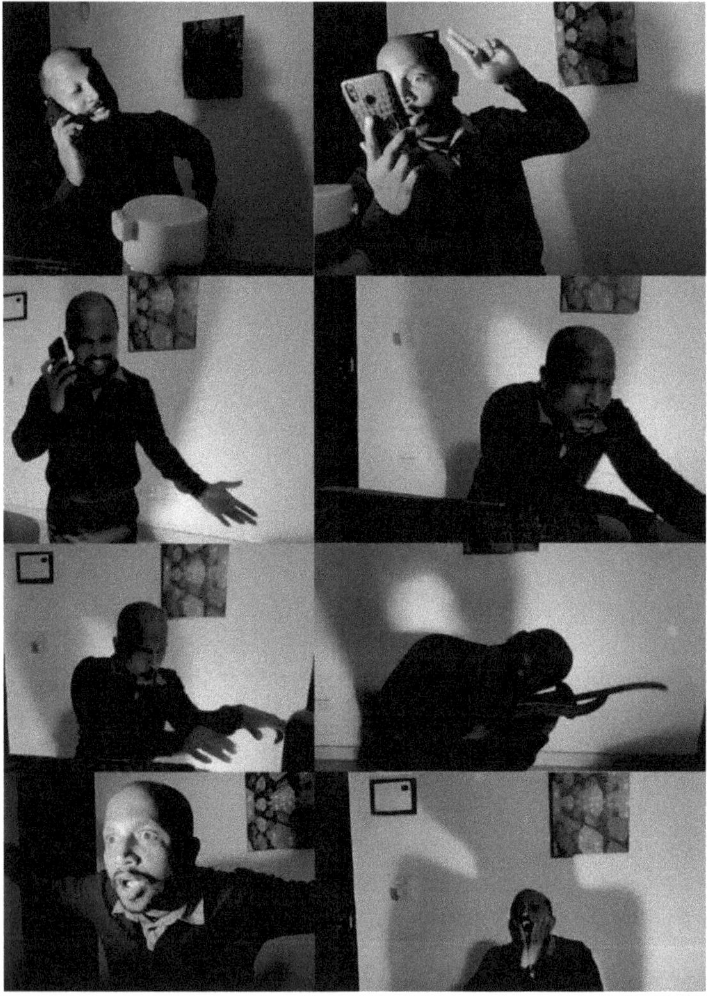

Figure 2: Transient emotions. *Source:* Printshot collage of "Carta 27 - Ephemeral"

(Sumesh PB, 2022).

This complex and ancestral system of acting and producing aesthetic flavor is used for many artists outside India, in a different or more simple way, looking for complimentary exercises of acting or even to discover possibilities forms of actuation. Shechner (2013) had developed a kind of game of emotions, based on Natya Shastra theory of *bhava* and *rasa*, called "Rasaboxes". According to his words:

For example, in workshops I led in the 1990s at New York University, I developed the rasaboxes exercise roughly based on the eight fundamental emotions described in the Natyasastra, the ancient Sanskrit manual for performers, directors, playwrights, and theatre architects.The rasaboxes exercise takes place inside a rectangle of nine boxes, each of which is the "place" of a basic emotion. As performers move from one box to the next, they must instantly change their emotional expression from, say, karuna (sadness or compassion) to bibhatsa (disgust), or raudra (rage), or sringara (love). But these words are not the key – each rasa is an entire range of feelings clustered around an emotional core, a flavoring and savoring of emotions rather than anything fixed or "texted." The aim of the exercise is to help performers compose, control, embody, and express emotions as nimbly as athletes are able to rest on the sidelines and then, when asked to play, plunge into the game with full intensity. Antonin Artaud once called for actors to be "athletes of the emotions," and this is what the rasaboxes exercise trains them to become (SCHECHNER, 2013, p. 233).

For many artists, theorists, and drama researchers the simple game that reduced Natya Shastra's ancestral art of performance is another cultural appropriation. The battle between European and American intercultural theorists who develop their theories on ancestral texts - or practices - is an old one, and Indian theorist Ruston Bharucha (1993) who questions this kind of interculturality:

If interculturalism in the theatre is to be more than a vision, there has to be a fairer exchange between theatrical traditions in the East and the West. At the moment, it is westerns who have initiated (and controlled) the exchange. It is they who have come to countries like India and take its rituals and techniques (either through photographs, documentation, or actual borrowings). The sheer poverty, if not destitution, of most performers in India clearly minimizes their possibilities of traveling to the West. Only a few Indian gurus and dancers have had the opportunity to visit European and American countries for lecture-demonstration and classes (BHARUCHA apud OKAMOTO; PETRONCARI, 2017, p. 38).

In the mid-1980s, Bharucha (1993) attacked Schechner's work, which quickly defended itself with a counterattack. This battle was published as an exchange of public letters and served to create a field of reflection and attention to otherness. Or at least think that there is always another side, as a coin or light/shadow construction.

One general observation that needs to be pointed out here is that none of the artists mentioned above [Richard Schechner, Gordon Craig, Jerzy Grotowski, Eugenio Barba, Peter Brook]- who represent, I might add, the most outstanding figures in the Euro-American theatre today – has turned to India out of the faintest concern for its present socio-cultural condition. Rather, they have been drawn almost exclusively to our 'traditional' sources (BHARUCHA, apud OKAMOTO; PETRONCARI, 2017, p.118).

Not only does Bharucha contest works based on cultural appropriation, but other artists who use the Schechnerian "Rasaboxes" method raise questions regarding the usefulness of the method/game. For Felluss (2020), founder and director of Theater Mundi's Jarjara Laboratory for Experimental Performance, California, USA, who used Rasaboxes to compose his authorial work, realized through his students/actors the spaces of blockage in the performance that the game brought:

My actors found it increasingly difficult to epistemologically "grasp" various emotional areas assigned on the stage. They seemed to lose stage presence at the moment they used the assigned affects. That is, the lines between rasas meant something, for as actors crossed them a jarring lapse occurred between their conception of the prefigured space and how their bodies "worked." The environment Schechner's Rasabox diagram mapped, while pioneering, was altogether too abstract, causing an immobilizing friction for my actors (FELLUS, 2020, p. 4).

If, on the one hand, there was a cultural appropriation by the so-called first world societies, on the other the work of these interculturalists reached me in the third world. At the time, he became the spokesman for Odissi dance in the West, promoting Odisha, the Natya Shastra, the gestures, the sinuous body and the expressions taught in the *gurukuls*. When today I wear my Odissi costume and make a public performance, whose side am I on?

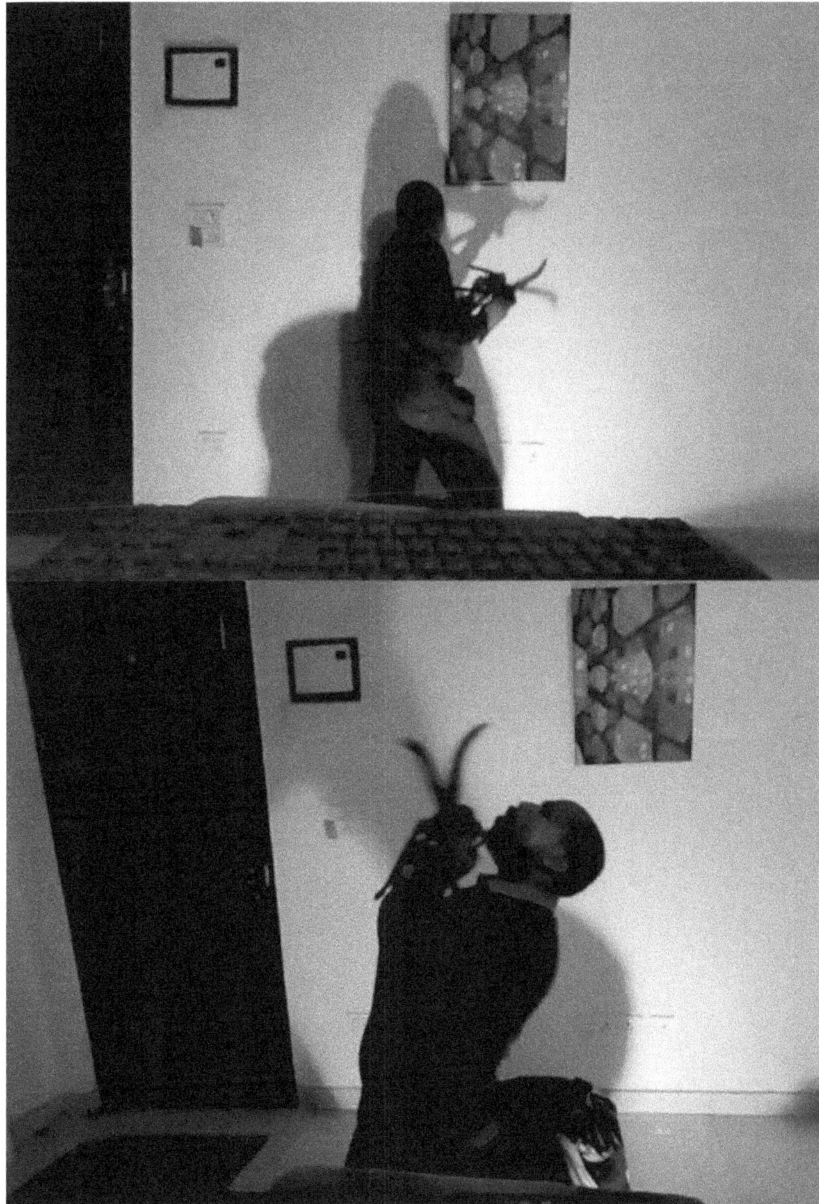

Figure 3: A battle of shadows and swords.

Source: Printshot collage of "Carta 27 - Ephemeral" (Sumesh PB, 2022.).

"Carta 27 - Ephemeral" contains the text of the performance, the non-verbal text, the text beyond the text itself. Schechner (1995) apud Barba (1991, p. 248) claims that "...the performance text is the whole multichannel process of communication that makes up a performative". The text used for this work is common to contemporary man surrounded by machines and technologies, and the internal struggles of self-control go through intimate battles of survival in society.

"Carta 27 - Ephemeral" is realistic, while it transcends reality, when emotions are expressed outside of cell phone dialogues. They appear in facial expressions, body gestures, but it is in the shadows that they swell and move towards a non-realistic universe or extra realistic composition. The different universes are directly connected to the two cell phones, which simultaneously call and interact with the actor. They bring the performance text and could be any kind of relation. Cell phones skillfully transform themselves into swords, whose shadows of an energetic and sonorous battle lead to the possibility of deep observation of the states of the soul. The cell phones in this work can be different types of relationships. They can also be two inner voices. They can be everything, including they can also bring about intercultural questions. While my own shadows and swords begin to dance ephemeral answers, I ask to myself: could my observation be my own intercultural performance text?

REFERENCES

BARBA, Eugenio. *A Dictionary of Theatre Anthropology*: The Secret Art of the Performer. Routledge, 1991.

BHARUCHA, Rustom. *Theatre and the world*: performance and the politics of culture. London: Routledge, 1993.

Carta 27 - Ephemeral. (Sumesh PB, 2022) Available in: https://www.youtube.com/watch?v=a1yp2bLHNVY . Accessed in: 12.jun.2023.

FELLUSS, Scott. Walking Rasic Space: A Critique of Schechner's "Rasaesthetics". In Liminalities: A Journal of Performance Studies, 16, No. 1. 2020.

JUNG, Gustav Carl. *Psychology and the Occult*. New York, Routledge, 2008.

SCHECHNER, Richard. *Performance Studies*: an introduction. New York, Routledge, 2013.

SCHECHNER, Richard. *The Performer:* training interculturally in between theatre and anthropology. University of Pennsylvania Press, 1985.

OKAMOTO, Eduardo; PETRONCARI, Vanessa. "Fricções culturais e criação cênica: Rustom Bharucha". In: Pitágoras, 7, n. 1, p. 110-122, [12], jan./jun. 2017. Available in: https://periodicos.sbu.unicamp.br/ojs/index.php/pit500/article/view/8650 805/16968 Accessed in: 12.jun.2023.

3

New Writings In Pandemic Times: Body And Technology (Letters 1, 9 & 26)

Cassiana Rodrigues Santana[5]

For a long time, I studied Indian dance from its "official" narratives. However, in recent years, especially with the advent of social networks and the expansion of "speech channels", this story has begun to be retold. It has always been questioned, but few were willing to give it due attention. Currently, we can hear many of these voices that claim their right to participate in history and that have been suffocated for decades, silenced within their own culture under the oppressive eyes of the ruling classes, which rewrite history according to their own interests. My involvement with intercultural studies happened through an intellectual path, through the emergence of issues and themes that have been widely discussed inside and outside the academy. However, it was fundamental in triggering a process that, perhaps, would never have been awakened had it not emerged from personal and collective pain.

Shifting this view to Brazil, it is possible to affirm that it is usually seen as a "mixed race, Christian and tolerant" country. This is how history has taught us, literature has validated, and the school curriculum has made it official. Discussing the problem that these three words carry would be a subject for research. However, for the purpose of this text, I will keep the focus on the experience that will be described, because, at this moment, I feel like I am rewriting the previous paragraph, changing the words, but not the situation. I don't mean to imply that we're talking about similar stories, because we're not. What I call into question are the vicissitudes of the so-called global south that intersect in several common points: in historical erasure, in prejudice, in subjugation. On the other hand, we also talk about resistance, connection with our roots and the desire for

---

5 Performer, PhD Scholar in the Performing Arts Graduate Program at Unicamp (advisor: Dr. Marilia Vieira Soares) and member of the research group Intercultural Studies in Performing Arts.

transformation that can no longer wait. We want to rewrite our history for what it is and not for what they want it to be and be recognized as a fundamental part of its construction. The colonization process is not over yet. The declarations of independence were not enough to decolonize the minds and bodies of the people, still tied to beliefs and ideals that never belonged to us and that were built to meet, as usual, foreign glances and institutions of power.

In 2020, in line with these reflections, I joined the research group "Intercultural Studies in Performing Arts" of the Department of Corporeal Arts of the University of Campinas, coordinated by Dr. Mariana Baruco M. Andraus. After a few meetings, we received the proposal to transform theoretical discussions into practice, or rather, into performance. To this end, we received an invitation to the scene through a creation-letter that brought some questions about our path at the university, our research and interest in intercultural studies. The letter also suggested objects and offered us the freedom to experiment with the path that best suited us, taking some questions as a reference, but opening ourselves up to any possibility. Considering the social isolation in which we still found ourselves, we would only have a cell phone and the space we could reach in such atypical circumstances, which eventually became a fertile field of creation.

Books, Flowers, and the Pestilence (Letter 1)

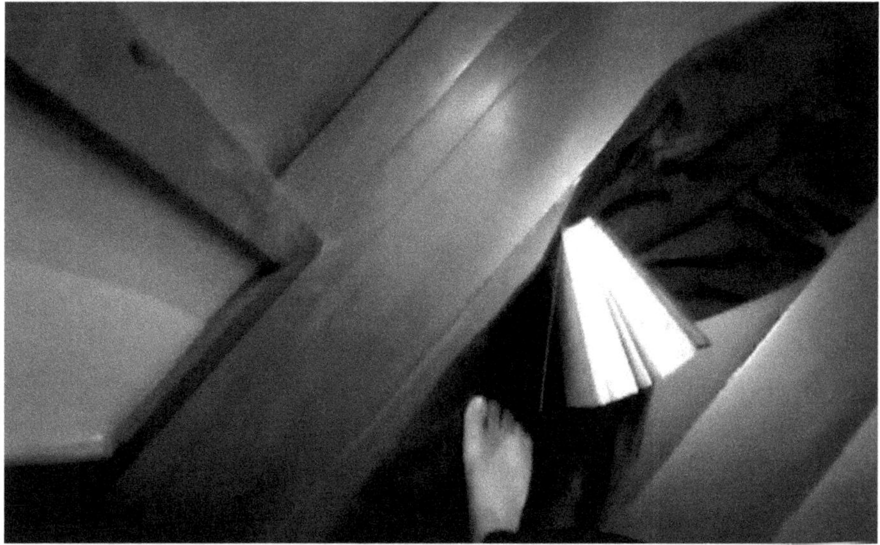

VIDEOPERFORMANCE: https://www.youtube.com/watch?v=NS-oP9YfVdE

My letter remained kept for some time in expectation of finding a narrative that would answer the questions it contained. I could not outline a movement, as answering these questions is the basis of my research and the reason for much anguish that accompanies the responsibility of answering them. I remember that when I read it for the first time, the only certainty I had was that I wanted to use a book and a red rose. But when picking it up again after some time, a sentence came to mind, bringing all the work back. She said: "this is not my story". That is what I wanted to answer for myself, for mine and for those who lived the same sense of historical nullification. From then on, many images crossed my mind, such as the desire to be among many books, to overthrow the "truths" they contained, and the stories built by the blood of many peoples and ethnicities. This blood that I chose to represent through a *saree*, a fabric about six meters long that, wrapped around the body, becomes the traditional garment of Indian women. When I chose a red *saree*, the color of my rose changed, as well as the choice of costume to wear.

At first, I thought of wearing a single-color outfit that could impose some neutrality on the exercise. A black outfit would be the most natural choice for me within what I learned in the theater as "training clothes", while white would remind me of the *terreiro* uniform (an area reserved for the rite in institutions that carry out spiritual works), since this was my reference. While I realized that both readings were personal and related to my experience, I also concluded that impartiality would be impossible in any cut I made, as it would always be delimited by some point of view. Everything that goes to the scene gains meaning through the viewer's experience and that is something that cannot be controlled. Everyday life, culture, ethnicity, space, climate, humor, everything participates in the filter that each one puts between what is shown, seen, and felt. Accepting the richness of this condition (because I do not see it as a limitation, but, on the contrary, I understand it as the enlargement of the scene by a plurality of perspectives), I surrendered to the impulses that arose, without trying to analyze each choice. I had the quoted sentence as a starting point and believed that everything else would follow. Furthermore, everything would start from movement, and I had already chosen books as the objects I wanted to relate to.

The sequence developed organically, as it exactly reproduced my feeling of being "in between", always going back and forth, not knowing where I was allowed to step, a feeling that was aggravated by intercultural research. This discomfort was also emphasized by the lack of space to move around, as I realized that the hallway of the apartment in which I found myself would be the ideal place to develop my scene. This narrow space gave me the feeling of suffocation that I felt in research. It gave me direction and limits, being also a place of passage, of crossing. A hallway is not considered a room, but a space between them and the one I was in gave me the possibility to choose the hidden paths between five closed doors. In addition, it was a place that anyone who chose to leave their room would need to cross. In fact, the word crossing was in the title of my master's thesis and this concept led all my previous research. Considering that I have my doctorate in progress, I still feel in that place where I realize that there are many doors that can be opened, but it is necessary to know which ones to choose.

Returning to the sequence, I chose to first reproduce my gaze, showing the path I was taking and the obstacles in it, represented by the books and their stories. Next, I positioned the camera in a panoramic perspective. Watching the video later, I realized that, in a way, I wanted to share with the viewer my research trajectory, expressed in unspoken words. I saw that every time I looked at the camera, I recognized the hidden presence of someone who would witness my choices. Firstly, tearing down what, for me, were fictional stories to wield power and manipulation, and secondly, redefining my path using those same stories to retell them through new looks. The movement of tearing down the books also provoked internal sensations that would certainly have been intensified if they had been more numerous and I had more time and space to repeat this action. However, circumstances not only shortened the sequence, but made me find the white rose at the end of the journey. I have no doubt I would like to bring down many more stories, but I think those spatial boundaries also have something to say. Perhaps this is a way of making me realize that it is no use there is no point in wanting to go beyond what I can achieve, and that it is necessary to take one step at a time, as finding balance in these new horizons is already a challenge enough for research in development.

The white rose, which came to work without much rationalization on my part, also took its place. It came as a brake, an offer of peace and a new beginning. She showed me that trying to erase what has been written in blood for so many centuries would be a waste of time and energy. I wouldn't be enough for a venture of this magnitude. It would be wiser and prudent to invest in writing new stories, rewriting others, making choices different from those imposed on me socially and politically. This rose showed me that I had the autonomy to undo my bonds, to release the book of my life from the pages I no longer want. Offering it to others would also be an invitation to rebuild relationships lost along questionable "truths". In my view, something far more productive than raising arms that would promote more strife and discord than reconciliation. We need no more bloodshed, no more bodies stretched out in history. We need more dialogue, to be open to hear other voices, languages, and experiences. I want more flowers than thorns, and to get them, I can only begin with myself.

Finally, I end my sequence with an improvised attitude, in an action that took precedence over thought, that of taking off the mask. The mask, a symbol of protection in a pandemic crisis, came to me through the image of those enslaved under the sign of torture, hunger, and silencing. The mask that can hide the face of evildoers, or punish those who crave for freedom, could not continue to exert its restraining force. I started my creation-letter with the phrase: "this is not my story". Therefore, if I intend to retell it, I need to get rid of everything that oppresses me, and I tried to do so using the symbols that were available to me.

So Many of Me (Letter 10)

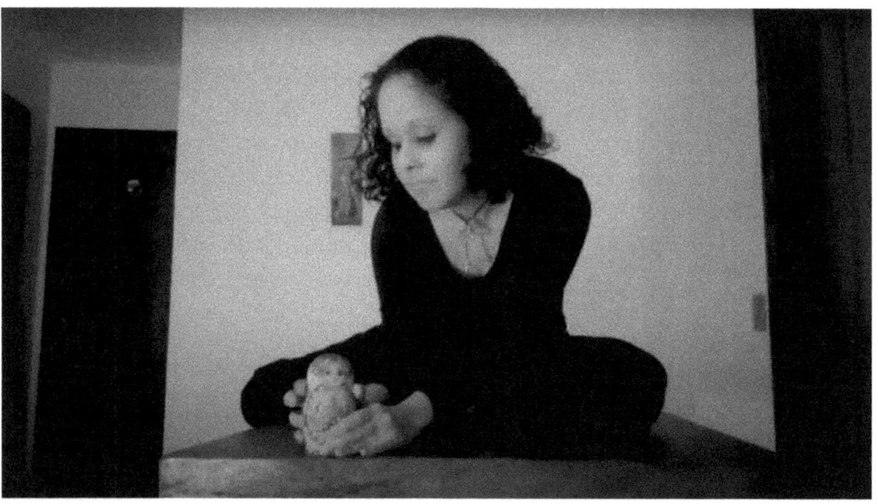

VIDEOPERFORMANCE: https://www.youtube.com/watch?v=M7CRM41qNDM

The second provocation that the group received was the proposal to tell a story, personal or invented, based on an object that affected us. At first, I looked for an object that would bring me memories, but maybe they were too present to be touched. I then came across a set of matryoshka dolls that I gained years ago from a person who knows well my enchantment for these Russian dolls. As a child I loved the idea of a doll that came out of another identical one, decreasing in size until it was no longer possible to reproduce their traits faithfully. While the idea of family to which the toy reminds me has always fascinated me, I see something imprisoning in this larger doll that guards, hides or arrests its counterparts. From this perception, many images and action verbs emerged that intersected among the women of this "family". I soon understood that it would not be a case of illustrating them, but of seeking, through these images, gestures, actions, emotions, and sensations that permeated them. But with a great differential, I could "break" these patterns, I had the key.

This vision was not immediate, on the contrary. I could only understand this when watching the finished sequence, where I could choose to "regurgitate" another woman from this family who, until then, had had her sequence/life interrupted. I also realized that I had a key around my neck, an object that I had chosen almost at randomly, but that has accompanied me for over twenty years in many scenes. When it jumped out at me, just before filming began, I didn't question it too much, I tied it on a ribbon and hung it around my neck. Since we were supposed to look for objects that affected us, there was one more, even if I could not rationalize it at that time.

Of all the sequences I worked on, this was the only one improvised from start to finish. I had only one situation, imprisonment, and one goal, set me free. However, the paths to it were open. I positioned the furniture I chose to use (it is worth mentioning that we were still in isolation from the pandemic), I picked the music that most motivated me at that moment and left for improvisation. Again, what guided me were the images and sensations that came both from the atmosphere imposed by the music and from the physically delimited space, a table, my prison, the one from which I needed to get out of. The scene reflected this search: attempts, giving up, fear, pain, pleasure... All the gestures and feelings were the open and closed paths that needed to be followed until the improvisation itself led me to a choice: to give an end to this endless repetition of patterns and self-imprisonments. However, that end would come through its opposition, through the choice of continuity, or rather, another way of moving forward.

From that moment on, I received a great contribution. The editing of this video was done by the same person who brought the proposal for this performance, Paula Ibañez, a researcher, and partner in this group. She multiplied these women, repeated, and reflected actions, brought another song, and re-signified even the simplest choices. It was also Paula who proposed the title "So many of Me", which gave a new meaning to everything I sought to transform through this improvisation and which, in her artistic sensitivity, she took beyond my expectations. Finally, I think we have reached common ground. Or rather, to a continuity, because the last doll cannot be eliminated from this lineage, it must be born to recreate these stories and give us back the smile that only change can bring. Even the video credits brought me this image, something that builds and falls apart in a continuous movement of coming and going. Nothing was discussed or decided between us. We just trust our processes and choose to dialogue through ways that are still little known and filtered by the technological universe. But when I saw so many images that cross me in the finished video, I could see how much our stories can connect us and how we can be an instrument of support and transformation in each other's lives. The performing arts imply collective action and what this work has shown us is that, even in times of seclusion, we are part of an inexhaustible network of possibilities.

Evelyn Roe (Letter 26)

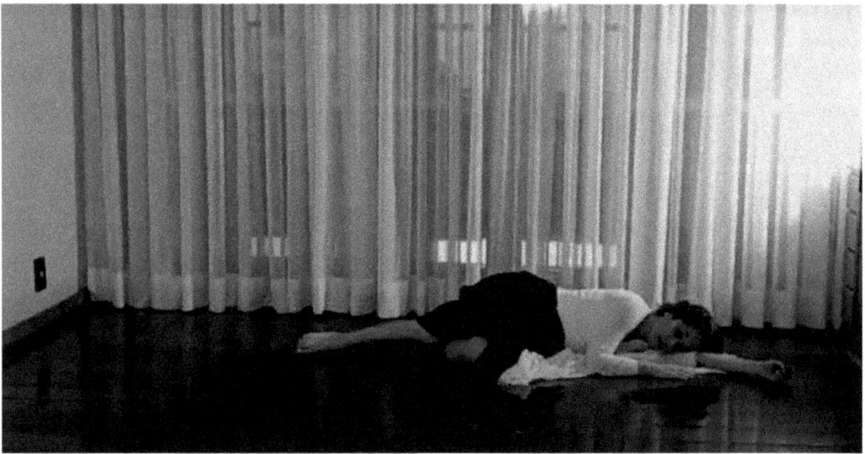

VIDEOPERFORMANCE: https://www.youtube.com/watch?v=cW7V9wzHC0k

The third proposal came from a fellow student at Pondicherry University, Aiswarya Lakshmi. G, and was perhaps the most challenging. She proposed to work on duality, which could easily lead us into a field of obviousness, but I had a long-standing creative block. I was thinking of several possibilities, including working with the oppositions of movement quality between the two styles of Indian dance I work with, Mohiniyattam and Kuchipudi. I research a lot about these oppositions, and it would be a natural way to go against them. But at the same time, I did not want to follow the known path. I sought duality in places that, perhaps, were less visible, but no less powerful. I had a lot of trouble finding this route and it was with the deadline for the delivery of the video approaching that, in a meditation, I remembered a poem that always moved me, "The legend of the prostitute Evelyn Roe", by Bertolt Brecht. I did not remember all the parts of the poem that I had worked with twenty years before, but I was sure that I had found the duality that I was looking for so much, because it wasn't in its protagonist, but in the look that the others had on her. For me, this was an inversion of paradigms, as it shifted the place of duality. The woman in the poem conveyed to me a certain purity in her essence, not as a moral quality, but as someone who had only one desire in life: to reach the Holy Land to "see Jesus Christ". The naivety with which she seeks this purpose causes her life to be transformed by the most varied forms of abuse, making her impure in the eyes of men, deities and, especially, herself. Ironically, only the devil could see her real soul.

This poem touches me in many instances because it calls into question fundamental discussion points in our society: the abuse against women (who are still held responsible for the violence they suffer), the discussion about religiosity, about heaven and hell, about the notions of morality, about what defines what makes someone good or bad, pure, or impure. This poem talks about hypocrisy, about silencing, about the loss of choices when the world chooses for you. Something that we live in a global dimension when we are defined by the gaze of others, by dominant groups that are distributed in different spheres: social, economic, religious, racial, etc. For me, Evelyn Roe is much more than a character who suffers from human injustice, she is a symbol recorded in a poem that can be unveiled in unimaginable and, dare I say, infinite layers. It will communicate with each society it passes through based on their own personal and collective experiences. This is where, for me, lies the beauty, wealth, and duality that I sought to work.

Realizing that the poem itself already contained all the oppositions I could wish for, it made no sense for me to illustrate it. I saw that everything I wanted could be found on this never-ending journey, personified by Evelyn Roe. I was no longer interested in the way she was seen, but in how those looks, and actions reached her through hope, joy, fear, abandonment, shame... I became interested in the seen and the unseen, in the emotions between the lines, in the circularity of time, in this place that never arrives. Even the music fulfilled this role. When choosing the poem, she came immediately after. "Light and Shadow", by Davide Martello, was the perfect sound for this spiraling image of a situation that repeats itself, however each time stronger and more harmful. The music conveyed playfulness and sadness with the same power. There was no other, it could not be another, it was it.

Another important point for me in this work was that, for the first time, I would edit the video myself. This greatly transformed my way of looking at the scenes, as I no longer in dialogue with a fellow student. My partners now were the poem and technology and that was challenging but also wonderful. I like working in a group, I like partnerships and going through all the stages of this work so lonely was a very different experience. On the other hand, looking back at the video later, it seemed to me that it made sense that it was so, as duality needed to be in the whole process. It was not something that was restricted to the scene, but to me as a creator, performer, and editor as well. As there was no other person to edit the video and be my double or opponent, I took that place in the choices I needed to make, as there were no preconceptions. Again, I worked from the images and sensations that the poem conveyed to me, but this time in a targeted way. There wasn't much room for improvisation because I knew where I wanted to go. Like Evelyn Roe, I stayed true to my intentions but without any control over their reception. I worked from the dualities that came my way, but those who will watch this video, belong to the look of each one. As well as each of the letters shared in this process crossed by so many researchers.

Partnership

Watching the videos of the study group I see very interesting aspects. As these processes were initiated during social isolation, we can see the solutions that each one found in their lives to deal with the proposal of the moment. Spatial limitations eventually provoked creative impulses that would hardly be triggered if not challenged, offering a wealth of possibilities. I realize that everyone opted for simplicity, investing more in their creative process than in large productions that could easily shift our attention from the performer to technology. It's great to have it as a partner, but not as the protagonist of the action.

Another point that caught my attention was the diversity of readings that each proposal brought, ranging from the structure of the scene itself to its editing features. The multiplicity of images that appeared among the participants was visible, especially in the videos that were put into dialogue without having been produced for that purpose. In some cases, two artists were placed in a relationship through the gaze of a third researcher who took care of the editing, taking the videos to unimaginable perspectives.

For me, nothing can replace the relationships that occur between the performer and the audience, and the video can be a harmful element to that relationship. However, during the pandemic, I discovered a very rich universe of work that, undoubtedly, transformed my outlook. For an artist-researcher it is important to never settle down, always being open to changes and new learning.

4

GRAMÁTICA – The Creative Process Of A Video Composition – Theoretical, Senses And Interculturality Poetic Through An Invitation Letter Proposal (Letter 3)

Andrea Albergaria[6]

Proposal and creation process from pandemic

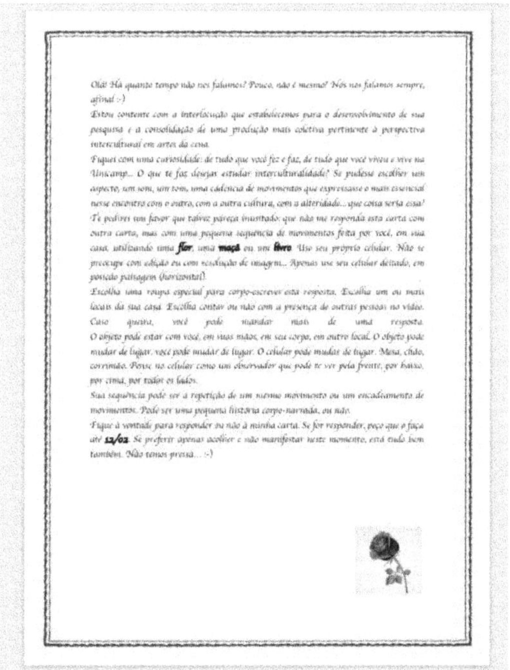

Olá! Há quanto tempo não nos falamos? Pouco, não é mesmo? Nós nos falamos sempre, afinal :-)

Estou contente com a interlocução que estabelecemos para o desenvolvimento de sua pesquisa e a consolidação de uma produção mais coletiva pertinente à perspectiva intercultural em artes da cena.

Fiquei com uma curiosidade: de tudo que você fez e faz, de tudo que você viveu e vive na Unicamp... O que te faz desejar estudar interculturalidade? Se pudesse escolher um aspecto, um som, um tom, uma cadência de movimentos que expressasse o mais essencial nesse encontro com o outro, com a outra cultura, com a alteridade... que coisa seria essa? Te peديrei um favor que talvez pareça inusitado: que não me respondia esta carta com outra carta, mas com uma pequena sequência de movimentos feita por você, em sua casa, utilizando uma **flor**, uma **maçã** ou um **livro**. Use seu próprio celular. Não te preocupe com edição ou com resolução de imagem... Apenas use seu celular deitado, em posição paisagem (horizontal).

Escolha uma roupa especial para corpo-escrever esta resposta. Escolha um ou mais locais da sua casa. Escolha contar ou não com a presença de outras pessoas no vídeo. Caso queira, você pode mandar mais de uma resposta. O objeto pode estar com você, em suas mãos, em seu corpo, em outro local. O objeto pode mudar de lugar, você pode mudar de lugar. O celular pode mudar de lugar. Mesa, chão, corrimão. Ponha no celular como um observador que pode te ver pela frente, por baixo, por cima, por todos os lados.

Sua sequência pode ser a repetição de um mesmo movimento ou um encadeamento de movimentos. Pode ser uma pequena história corpo-narrada, ou não.

Fique à vontade para responder ou não à minha carta. Se for responder, peço que o faça até **12/02**. Se preferir apenas acolher e não manifestar neste momento, está tudo bem também. Não temos pressa... :-)

Figure 1: Creation letter in the pandemic - invitation. Source: Printshot from Invitation Creation Letter (2021).

6 Odissi dance teacher, Phd Scholar in the Performing Arts Graduate Program at Unicamp (advisor: Dr. Mariana B. M. Andraus) and member of the research group Intercultural Studies in Performing Arts.

To answer the letter[7] sent by Prof. Mariana Andraus, first effective proposal for an artistic composition, whether in duos or collectives, within the study group intercultural groups that we are all part of and composed of members from different areas and languages, I describe some stages inserted in my individual creative process, and that resulted in the video *GramÁtica*. I emphasise here the specificity of my specialty artistic, based on training in Indian Odissi dance, which is the theme of deepening my doctoral research, and which, therefore, permeates my scenic investigations regarding locomotion and spaces.

At first, the letter provoked strange reactions, not because of the proposal, but because it brought objects that maybe I didn't want to have contact with. Although the three of them literally sharpened my senses: a flower, an apple, or a book, either by the real everyday presence of items common foods, or even by inducing the olfactory, palatal, visual and sensorial memories of some species, as potent catalysts of creative actions, their lack of definition caused in I was suddenly repulsed and left the provocation at bay. They could then be in a garden, in a fruit basket and on a shelf. Subjective or real places that at that moment did not I could access. What garden, and what perfume could a flower exude? An apple, green or red, whole, or already bitten? And any book or my own, recently published and at the same time not so consistent with my current research. As a task to be fulfilled, I wanted to get in touch with the letter, with the referred objects, which were not mandatory in their use, just as the answer itself was not. The letter was a subtle invitation to dive, and while she proposed, she left it free for nothing to happen again. Your spaces for creation were there, in the vagueness of objects, in the possibilities of refusal, and so the game had started. If rationally I could not access these spaces for compose, in dreams I answered the letter, which in a dreamlike way came in an envelope, and I replied, writing in pencil, feeling the texture of the paper

---

7 *Creation Letter* in English version: "Hey you! I'm very glad to know you. I'm happy we connected to develop an artistic project that may turn to research production in the future. Let's start from the basis: could you create a simple sequence of movements, between one or two minutes, using a flower, an apple or a book, to tell me what you think we can exchange between Brazilian and Indian culture, myths and/or symbolisms? Use your own cell phone (please record horizontally) and make it preferentially at your home. You can dance, act or even use martial arts movements. It will be all nice. I just want to know you better by the things your movements tell me. Choose special clothes to write this answer. Choose one or more places at your house. The chosen object can be with you, in your hands, in your body or other place. The object can move to other places, you can move to other places. The cell phone can also move to other places. Tables, floor, stairs... Consider the cell phone as an observer that can see you from the front, from the bottom, from the top and/or every side. Your sequence can be the repetition of the same movement or the organisation of different movements. It can also be a short story that you tell me with your body. You can answer or not my letter... If you want to answer, I will ask you to do it by March 10th. And, if you don't want to answer, it will be ok too! (2021).

and the sound produced by this friction of my hand on the paper, along with that of the graphite that slid in curves, points, different lines on a blank sheet. There was a rhythm to this writing, which when awakened found it when rereading the proposed letter. From the letter in Portuguese language version, I highlight below, in bold, the phrases, pauses, expressions that caught my attention and that resulted in the soundscape that I used for editing the *GramÁtica* response video:

Portuguese:

Olá! Há **quanto** tempo não nos falamos? **Pouco**, não é mesmo? Nós nos falamos **sempre**, afinal :-) **Estou** contente com a interlocução que estabelecemos para o desenvolvimento de **sua** pesquisa e a consolidação de uma produção mais coletiva pertinente à perspectiva intercultural em artes da cena. **Fiquei** com **uma** curiosidade: de **tudo** que você **fez** e **faz**, de **tudo** que você **viveu** e **vive** na Unicamp... O que **te faz desejar** estudar interculturalidade? **Se pudesse** escolher **um** aspecto, **um** som, **um** tom, **uma** cadência de movimentos que expressasse o **mais** essencial nesse encontro **com o outro, com a outra** cultura, com a **alteridade**... que coisa seria essa? **Te pedirei um** favor que talvez pareça inusitado: que **não** me responda esta carta com **outra** carta, mas com **uma** pequena sequência de movimentos feita por você, em **sua** casa, utilizando **uma** flor, **uma** maçã ou **um** livro. Use **seu** próprio celular. **Não** se preocupe **com** edição ou com resolução de imagem... **Apenas** use seu celular deitado, **em** posição paisagem (horizontal). **Escolha uma** roupa especial para corpo-escrever esta resposta. **Escolha** um **ou mais** locais da sua casa. **Escolha** contar **ou não** com a presença de outras pessoas no vídeo. **Caso** queira, você **pode** mandar **mais de uma** resposta. O objeto **pode** estar com você, em suas mãos, em seu corpo, em outro local. O objeto **pode** mudar de lugar, você **pode** mudar de lugar. O celular pode mudar de lugar. Mesa, chão, corrimão. **Pense** no celular como um observador que pode te ver **pela frente, por baixo, por cima**, por todos os lados. Sua sequência pode ser a repetição de um mesmo movimento ou um encadeamento de movimentos. Pode **ser um**a pequena história corpo-narrada, **ou não**. Fique **à** vontade para responder ou não **à** minha carta. **Se** for responder, **peço** que o faça até 12/02. **Se** preferir apenas **acolher** e não manifestar neste momento, está **tudo** bem também. Não **temos** pressa... (Invitation Creation Letter, Andraus, 2021).

English:

Hello! How long has it been since we spoke? **Little**, right? We **always** talk, after all :-) **I am** happy with the dialogue we established for the development of **your** research and the consolidation of a more collective production pertinent to the intercultural perspective in performing arts. **I was** curious: **everything** you **did** and **do, everything** you **experienced** and **are living** at Unicamp... What **makes you want** to study interculturality? **If you could** choose **an** aspect, **a** sound, **a** tone, a cadence of movements that expressed the **most** essential thing in this **encounter with the other, with the other culture, with otherness**... what would that be? **I will ask you** a favor that may seem unusual: that you **do not** answer this letter with **another** letter, but with **a** small sequence of movements made by you, in **your** home, using **a** flower, **an** apple or **a** book. Use **your own** cell phone. **Don't** worry **about** editing or image resolution... **Just** use your cell phone lying down, **in** landscape (horizontal) position. **Choose a** special outfit to body-write this answer. **Choose** one **or more** locations in your home. **Choose** whether **or not** to count on the presence of other people in the video. **If** you wish, you **can** send **more than one** response. The object **may** be with you, in your hands, on your body, in another location. The object **can** change place, you **can** change place. The cell phone can change location. Table, floor, handrail. **Think** of your cell phone as an observer that can see you **from in front**, from **below**, from **above**, from all sides. Its sequence can be the repetition of the same movement or a chain of movements. It can **be** a short body-narrated story, **or not**. Feel free to respond or not **to** my letter. **If** you are going to respond, **I ask** that you do so by 12/02. **If** you prefer to just **welcome** and not express it at this time, that's okay too. We are in no rush... (Invitation Creation Letter, Andraus, 2021).

Once, twice, maybe many times, I don't remember exactly how many times I heard my voice reading the text in its entirety. But the letter, in this almost dramatic reading, had a time marked by the words arranged in the textual body. Some words were strong, and seriously stood out in my reading. Such words, loose, sonically created a kind of rhythmic phrase, and thus turning into a sound I'm used to, a splint of Indian dance and music, provoked access to creative spaces. The splints, originally composed of small sound syllables, time stamping, base rhythm for the melody played by instruments, by the voice, or by the sound of the wind, the breath of air, arose from the words written in the letter. They surfaced like musical scores for the cycles of Indian art, dance, theatre, singing, recitation and with them I recorded a soundtrack on my cell phone reading the chosen words, creating a new text from the original one, as a concrete poem. For this literary movement that emerged in the twentieth century in Europe and had a significant importance in Brazilian literature, founded by Brazilian *Noigandres Concrete Poetry Group* (1952-1962) "...the writer of *concrete poetry* uses typeface [...] in such a way that chosen units—letter fragments [...], graphemes (letters) syllables, or words" (BRITANNICA, 2019) to create a space that changes a single meaning of each word or phrase. This can also be considered a *sound poem*, where meaning only emerged through voice reading or recording, causing different sound effects or rhythms, provoking other meanings or none.

"olá

quanto pouco sempre estou

sua fiquei

uma tudo fez faz

tudo viveu vive te faz desejar

se pudesse

um um um uma

mais

com o outro com a outra

alteridade

te pedirei um

não outra uma sua uma uma um seu

não com apenas em escolha

uma escolha ou mais escolha

ou não

caso pode mais de uma

pode pode pode

pense pela frente

por baixo

por cima

ser uma ou não

à

à

se peço

se acolher tudo temos

barra reticências dois pontos fecha parênteses"* [8]

---

8 My concrete poem emerged from original letter: "hello/ how little I am always /yours I stayed/ one everything did does/ everything lived lives makes you wish/ if I could/ one one one one/ more /with the other (him) with the other

As a sound poem, *Taal*, the Indian rhythm cycle with its sonorous syllables, also always provokes curiosity and estrangement for an outsider, like me. It begins with the first clap and runs through syllables and claps, under various ways other houses of time, in counting the splints, it ends in the first house. For being cyclical, this structure goes back and forth, in different possibilities: it bends, slows down, grows, decreases, travels, ascends, fixes, dissolves, descends, circulates within itself, expands, hesitates, slides and returns to its beginning. The study of this complex system, so different from our western musical conception, is at least a rich sound universe to be transformed into danced poetry. The words of the letter, like a sound score, led me in movements and I went through all the houses of an imaginary cycle, where those and other objects became ornaments for my occupation in the melody of silence, where I inserted myself as a microbody and carried them and walked through the macro body of my house. *GramÁtica* emerges like this, as response video, permeated by sound layers that stimulate body composition, determined by the constant presence of Indian art concepts already internalised in my way of investigating art, and whose foundations, so present in its structural bases codified and millenary, provide in a mobile and cyclical way the spatial filling to the add new possibilities to our own ancestry.

The Grammars

The words could be read as a new poetry, a concrete poetry, but even so, more than their meaning, the idea of a void in the pandemic moment when the interactive proposal was made - question/answer, said more than any literality. This void, a suspended state in which we all found ourselves, was the initial investigation site. It was thus possible to build the poetics of the moment through the senses, observations, and my own work tools awakened by the provocation of the letter. The swivel chair was the starting point for the investigation of a walk, towards the search for such objects, or the sensations they could bring. Spinning around, I came across my feet, floating, fast, without ground. How could they land on solid ground? What does it look like to me when I turn around and see my feet trying to settle? I see what I can see, some extracts from a studied corporal grammar. Both Aristotle's Poetic and Bharata Muni's Natya Shastra were references present in the process of creating *GramÁtica*. Penna (2017) about Aristotle's Poetic states that:

(her)/ otherness/ I will ask you one/ no other one your one one one your/ no with only in choice/ a choice or more choice/ or not /if you can more than one/ can can can/ think from the front/ under/ the top /to be one or not /to/ to/ if I ask /if you accept everything we have/ an ellipsis/ slash/ a colon/ closes parentheses" (approximately translation).

The founding element of poetic poetry, in general, will be precisely the fact that, through words, sounds, expressions and gestures, something, actions, experiences, passions, characters, etc. Moreover, the essentially "productive" aspect of poetics, which is to awaken the pleasure (hedoné) inherent in the tragic feeling (pathos) of terror (phóbos) and piety (Éleos) (PENNA, 2017, p. 55).[9]

A sequence of foot postures that determine the mechanics of walking, jumping, running, fleeing are described in Chapter XII of the ancient treatise on Indian dance, the Natya Shastra (Bharata Muni, II B.C.). The feet, as well as other parts of the body, receive meticulous detail as to the possible uses to compose a dance, whether interpretive or not. There are 36 postures of feet, described under the title *Pada Bheda*, and integrated as a Natya Shastra chapter and guide for artist training of classical Indian dances learning. According to SINGH (2019), about Natya Shastra, body division parts are present on "[...] The chapters like 8, 9, 10, 11 and 12 codify body language based on a definite semiotics" and this can be applied to the motion of a scene composition. Singh (2019) further claims that:

The Natyashastra's primary concerns are not philosophical or theoretical; rather, the text elucidates and elaborates how theatre is performed. It prescribes in detail the construction of theatre spaces in India, the application of make-up, the design and building of props, arm, foot, eye and other body movements, ritual practices, the organization of theatre companies, the audience, dramatic competitions and the community of actors with additional chapters on music and audience appreciation. It elaborates the affectiveness of theatre (SINGH, 2019, p. 90).

The grammars or the systems that create methodologies are indicators of possibilities, they are determined agreements between creator and interpreter, with the consent of the public. But after some time that order can be reversed, the audience demands the grammar, and the creator replicates what the interpreter is doing. When the creator is the interpreter and also his own audience, these agreements occur simultaneously, and disorderly. And in the chaos of disorder, a propitious place for creation and discovery, other readings of old grammars may appear. This new view does not change the grammar, it is simply a different form of observation.

---

9 From original: "[...] o elemento fundante da poesia poética, em geral, será justamente o fato de que, por meio de palavras, sons, expressões e gestos, se mimetiza algo, ações, experiências, paixões, caracteres etc. Além disso, o aspecto essencialmente "produtivo" da poética, que é despertar o prazer (*hedoné*) inerente ao sentimento trágico (*páthos*) de terror (phóbos) e piedade (*éleos*)" (PENNA, 2017, p. 55).

Those who strictly follow the grammar will not feel offended or harmed, as they know that it is a place of common sense that the outsider's eye was able to see. And that look doesn't mean front or threat. And for the thinking outsider, this way of seeing and feeling the method creates meaning for the understanding of the method itself and thus he manages to enter into common sense.

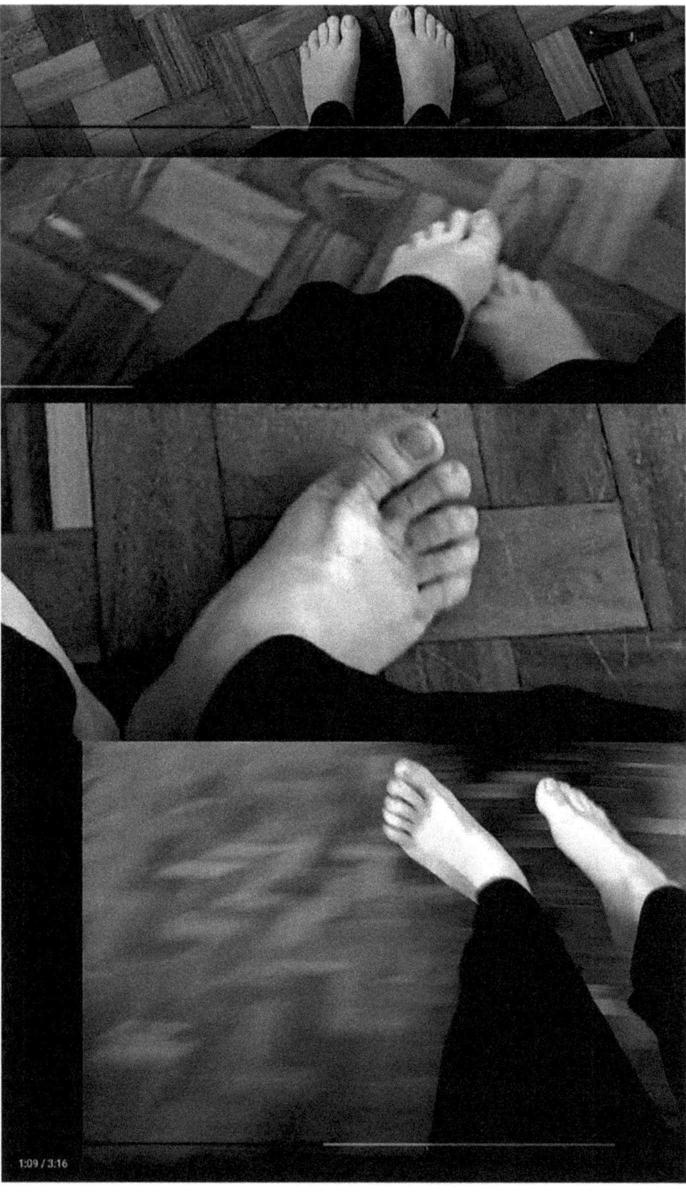

Figure 2: *Padha Beda:* Odissi dance foot grammar. Source: Printshot of *GramÁtica* (2022).

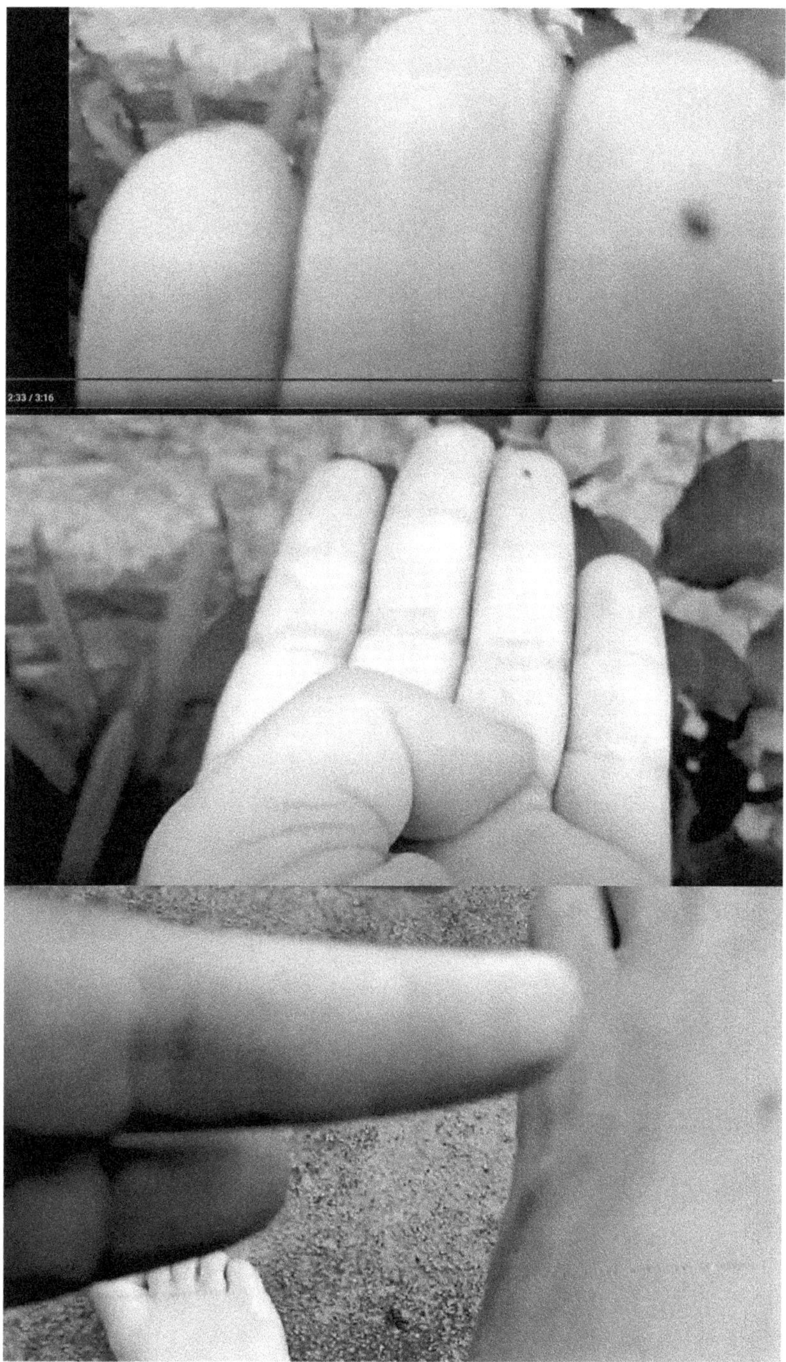

Figure 3: *Hasta Mudra Viniyoga*: hand gestures grammar. Source: Printshot of *GramÁtica* (2022).

For Arendt, apud Sorgel (2019, p.99), there are two ways of seeing the world: the first in a rational way, where objects perform their functions, and the second in a way disassociated from the purpose or function of that object or situation. Like this, Arendt (1981) relates Aristotle's thought about the *bios xenicos* or the foreign being, as a way for creative process. The look of the outsider is the look of someone who is always in a kind of absence of reality, however, for the sake of survival, it is in this reality, in this common sense, he (she) finds himself (herself) and inserts himself (herself):

These we call philosophers, and their way of life will always be "the life of a stranger" (bios xenicos), as Aristotle called in his Politics. And the reason that strangeness and absent-mindedness are not more dangerous, that all "thinkers", professionals and laymen alike, survive so easily the loss of the feeling of realness, is just that the thinking ego asserts itself only temporarily: every thinker no matter how eminent remains "a man like you and me" (Plato), an appearance among appearances equipped with common sense and knowing enough common-sense reasoning to survive ARENDT, 1981, p. 49).

The deconstructed text brought to light a character, who was perhaps myself, in that moment of isolation from the pandemic, with so many parallels and experiencing recent grief. Objects like the flower, the apple and the book did not emerge in this sieve of words, and reservoirs of pain, fear, sadness and lack of perspective were obtained. And that's how they entered the scene.

Art therefore, which transforms sense-objects into thought-things, tears them first of all out of their context in order to de-realize and thus prepare them for their new and different function (ARENDT, 1981, p. 49).

Objects and approaches

Only the lonely, fragmented, and lost character emerged with the fragmentation of the creation card, and it was from her that I started building the scene. At first, the loneliness and lack of ground, the feeling of not being in the world, or at least in a world that I had once known. The turn in the chair and the flight of the feet expressed that moment. With a lot of effort, I started walking. In the beginning, in the room itself, a safe place, where the virus would not enter. Opening the door was dangerous, and even alone I followed the loose words of the letter. To tiptoe down the stairs, touch the rose, withered, already practically dead, and pierce my hand with the thorn of its stem: the blood oozing softly along with a piercing pain. And my feet having to move forward, leading my body. It would be the dance of death, the dance of life, the dance of mourning: All dances of survival, of rites, and therefore ornamented feet painted with drops of my blood, instead of the usual *alta*. Withered petals as offering to unknown dance.

Even though the proposed objects were not initially used by me, because with my senses awake, what stood out in the creation process were the body grammars and the letter. All objects appeared at the end of the video, agglutinated in the same initial seated posture in the swivel chair. Both the flower, already plucked, and the bitten apple, and the book, being read by the absence of vision, since my eyes were tied, awakened the impossibility of the function of the senses or even the alteration of their function. The apple, unwillingly bitten, the withered petals and the unread book brought the moment of the impossibilities and uncertainties of the pandemic, together with the feet shod in shoes that would lead nowhere.

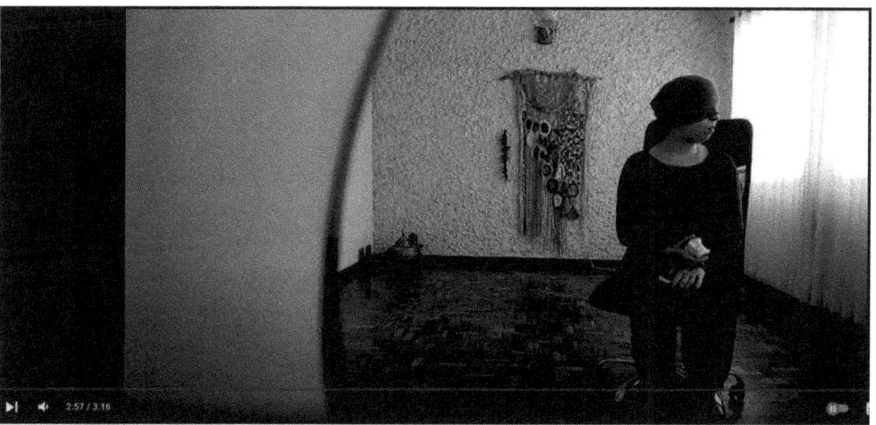

Figure 4: As Tiresias: the wise blind prophet and the uncertain future. Source: Printshot of video *GramÁtica* (2022).

[...] (enters TIRESIAS, guided by a boy)

TIRESIAS - Oh theban bosses, we, who are here, made a long journey together! One of us sees for the other; Well, you know that blind people cannot walk without a guide (in Antigone of Sophocles)[10] (Sophocles; Ésquilo, 1992, p.99).

Over the months, the different proponents and recipients created their artistic proposals and responses. In addition to having participated in all the proposals, I was able to observe, as a member of the group, an interactivity that was moulding, solidifying, intertwining throughout the meetings and works produced. The group, even without face-to-face contact, acquired the character of a group, which is belonging, the place of common sense. We all created a way of working, which was perceived and felt with each new production. As an intercultural group all of us were in a game of question and answer, and we always left online meetings, at least, being touched for a different observation or result expectation. Famous about his published works on intercultural performing arts field, Rustom Bharucha (1995), in his work *Chandralekha: Woman, Dance, Resistance,* he reports that Chandralekha (1928 - 2006) was someone who has been naturally open for get communication, no matter language, religion or nationality. As an artist, she was very conscious about herself and how to be in the world, as a rootedness being, but out of closed minds groups and regionalism. She made a revolution with her compositions on Indian dance, emerged from her Bharat Natyam background and to add martial arts in her compositions. According to Bharucha (1995, p. 32) "[...] Chandra was content to uphold the simple truth that art helps us to cope with life".

A confrontation of the 'grammar' of dance is both necessary and difficult because it exposes those very traps and deceptions that one acquires through performance. Besides, the 'fundamentals' of dance reveal the richest sources of poetry in the language of the body. 'What they call grammar,' as Chandra says of her detractors, 'is poetry to me.' (BHARUCHA, 1995, p. 153).

Final consideration

The Treaties of Muni and Aristoteles were only highlighted by the issue of affectivity, memory, and the possibilities that both bring to the proposed response of the creation letter, and by the bridge that both form between India and the West, in terms of the performing arts. That same bridge, crossed by so many scholars, artists, researchers over time, is also a place of non-place.

Working with the intercultural group was both to confront grammars, not in the sense of validation of knowledge, but in the sense of an understanding that what we did (we, Brazilians with formation in different dances of India) was also Indian dance, even without to be. And sometimes, I found myself confronting my way of understanding Indian dance in my own body, and that was what had the most value in the creation process. Without the costume, without the music, without the narrative, without the bells, without makeup, no flowers in the head, how much of the Odissi dance was in me? Maybe no one saw what I felt: the Odissi technique was a place of passage and also something that passed me. Thus, like Aristotle *bio xenicos*, I could come out of reality to create, and yet, with the eye of the abroad to see in another way what would be common sense.

REFERENCES

ARENDT, H. *The life of the mind.* New York: Mariners Book, 1981.

BHARUCHA, R. *Chandralekha;* Woman, Dance Resistance. An imprint of HarperCollins Publishers India, New Delhi, 1995.

BRITANNICA. The Editors of Encyclopaedia. *"concrete poetry".* Encyclopedia Britannica, 8 Mar. 2019, https://www.britannica.com/art/concrete-poetry. Accessed 22 February 2023.

GRAMÁTICA. Available at: https://www.youtube.com/watch?v=LkiWE-SKW9o&t=69s Accessed on 18/02/2023.

PENNA, Tiago. A poética de Aristóteles: conceito e racionalidade. João Pessoa, Tese de Doutorado em Filosofia. Programa integrado UFPB/UFPE/UFRN/CCHALA, 2017. Available at: https://repositorio.ufpb.br/jspui/bitstream/123456789/12029/1/Arquivototal.pdf Accessed on 25/02/2023.

SINGH, M. R. Bharat Muni's Natyashastra: a comprehensive study. International Journal of English Language, Literature and Translation Studies (IJELR) India, Vol 6 Issue1. (Jan-March). 2019. Available at: https://www.lkouniv.ac.in/site/writereaddata/siteContent/2020041206321 94475nishi_Natyashastra.pdf Accessed on 27/02/2023.

SÓFOCLES; ÉSQUILO. (Tradução J.B. Mello e Souza). *Rei Édipo Antígone Prometeu Acorrentado* - Coleção Clássicos de Bolso - RJ, Ediouro, 1992.

SÖRGEL, Sabine. The interweaving of movement cultures in Gregory Maqoma's Beautiful Me. *In: Movements of Interweaving Dance and Corporeality in Times of Travel and Migration.* Edited by Brandstetter, G; Egert, G. and Hartung, H. Routledges, London, New York, 2019.

5

Crossing Borders: Intercontinental Creative Partnerships Through The Use Of Technology And Asynchronous Creation Procedures (Letters 5, 11, 15, 21, 25)

Mariana Baruco Machado Andraus

The transposition of creative processes to remote versions has become a research topic in the performing arts with greater emphasis since the covid-19 pandemic confined artists from all over the world to their homes (Andraus, 2021; Manzolli, Andraus, 2021). At the same time that confinement brought limitations, it can be said that, on the other hand, there is a crossing border that ended up being facilitated through the use of technologies, especially the Google Meet tool, which enables meetings between researchers from any place on the planet without the usual commitments of time and financial resources involved in a trip, and video editing software that has become a working tool for performing artists who previously were not familiar with this type of resource.

In the research group Intercultural Studies in Performing Arts, a dynamic of creative partnerships was established through these resources, always triggered by letters that proposed artistic actions. Despite my participation in practically all the videos available on the channel so far – either as an action proponent, in the conception of scripts for video editing (and the technical edition itself) or as a performer –, in this chapter I make an excerpt to write specifically about my work as a creator and performer in five videos: I. Epifania - Primeiro Movimento; II. Oxumaré hugs me every morning; III. Dust Cloud; IV. Healing waters; and V. Dual, which correspond, respectively, to Letters 5, 11, 15, 21 and 25. In these videos I participated as a creator and performer and I have elements to discuss the symbolic choices that permeated the imagery and musical references, placing them in perspective with my own story as an artist-creator. In the end, I will make general comments on the experience of the partnership, which, by the way, has always proved to be enriching for my continuing education as an artist and researcher of the performing arts.

I. Epiphany - First Movement (Letter 5)

The videoperformance "Epifania – Primeiro Movimento" was my response to the artistic action proposed by researcher Paula Ibañez, presented by her in the following text:

Once upon a time there was a scarf, a perfume, a brooch, a button. Once upon a time there was a dry flower selfishly kept in the middle of a book. Once upon a time there was a broken fan, a photo, a lock of hair tied with a red ribbon to avoid the evil eye. A doll, a pebble, a note.

Each one of them with their story, with my story. Real or imagined, it doesn't matter.

This letter is an invitation for you to immerse yourself in your stories, for you to choose an affectation object that is yours and tell us your story. What it was or what you imagined; it doesn't matter.

Tell us, however you want and if you want.

If you accept this invitation, please send us your video-letter-reply by 04/10, on my private WhatsApp or via a sharing link, also in private. Thanks! (Proposal for an artistic action prepared by Paula Ibañez on March 10, 2021).

Based on the proposal to create a scene inspired by an affection object that told a little of our stories, I chose a pebble tree that is a decorative object in my house and that says a lot about the mystical side that I have cultivated since my youth, and which is very connected to the religion I practice: umbanda.

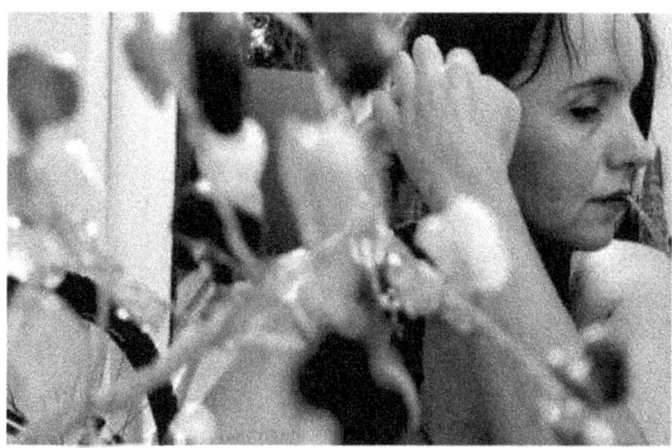

VIDEOPERFORMANCE: https://www.youtube.com/watch?v=MjDWmt08nGo

Umbanda is an Afro-Brazilian religion based on the cultural syncretism of different people and ethnicities that currently constitute the population that recognizes itself as Brazilian: African people of different origins (Bantu, Yoruba, Jêje, among others), native Brazilian peoples (indigenous people) and, in the case of European immigrants, especially the Portuguese who colonized Brazil throughout the 16th to 19th centuries, but also Italian immigrants who arrived in Brazil between the 19th and 20th centuries. The religion Umbanda is based on the incorporation of spirits in the form of *caboclos* (or indigenous people), *pretos-velhos* (Africans enslaved in the colonisation period), children (or *eres*, or *ibejis*) and the *exus* and *pombagiras*, entities more connected to material life. In each *terreiro*, these "categories" can diversify and unfold into other subcategories, such as "sailors", "cowboys", among others. There is no institutional instance that centralizes and normalizes rules on the foundations of this religion and, therefore, each *terreiro* enjoys the freedom to self-determine and establish its own rules.

My experience of twenty-six years as a practitioner of this religion took place always in the same *terreiro*, which is organized into seven spiritual lines: Oxalá, Oxossi, Ogum, Xangô, Iemanjá, Pretos-Velhos, Xangô Caô (this last is equivalent to what is called "Eastern Line" in other *terreiros*). They are respectively syncretized with Jesus, Saint Sebastian, Saint George, Saint Jerome, Maria (Jesus mother), Saint Cyprian and Saint John the Baptist, in the Catholic liturgy. In order not to dwell on the liturgical explanations and going straight to the point, in the video "Epifania - Primeiro Movimento", when choosing the stones as an object, I looked for the reference of the orixá Xangô, which led me to choose to wear orange pants for the performance.

At that time, I used short hair and my image resembled that of an older woman. Then came the movement in which I slowly tip my body towards the ground, as if I were falling or lying down, tired, throwing my arms up and with tight lips, as if in a breath. The slowness of this sequence contrasts with the accelerated beat chosen by Paula Ibañez (Agueré de Oxossi), who, in dialogue with me, defined the concept and edited the video.

Another Umbanda element present in this video is the Espada de São Jorge plant (or Espada de Ogum, another orixá), in front of which I did the whole performance. In the side corridor of my house, I have a flowerbed full of this plant, which is often used for protecting infusions. In the videoperformance, at minute 1:54 I begin to explore movements with my left arm passing between the Swords of Saint George as if it were a serpent. In doing so, I occasionally make configurations with my hand in the form of some mudras – gestures learned in the study of Indian Odissi dance.

These moments are interspersed with the throwing of pebbles on the floor, based on a popular game called Amarelinha, in which children draw a path on the floor with chalk and, following a series of rules, hop along this path with only one foot.

Then, like a mother gathering toys after an afternoon of playing with the children, I walk down the hall picking up the pebbles, one by one, as a reference to motherhood, to a woman who takes care of, who organizes spaces.

As I was working with various "earth" elements – that is, firm, stable, linked to old age, maturity – I chose to oppose, in terms of movements, some scenes with tremors. I held the pebble tree with the soles of my feet and started to shake with my feet, so that the pebbles were agitated, and I also captured images of the swords of Saint George being shaken by my hands.

I noticed the handles of two red flowers in a cross and decided to focus on them with the camera, as they reminded me of the image of Xangô's double ax (Oxé de Xangô) that devotees of this deity hang in their homes as an object of protection. One of the flowers was under a stone and I found this image composition interesting, as both the crossed cables and the stone are elements of this orixá (that is what it represents for me).

Towards the end, another plant widely used in Umbanda appears, the rue, whose image I capture above and begin to explore postures with the feet also studied in the Indian Odissi dance (and, in editing, these images sometimes overlap with the images of mudras). On the other hand, this foot posture that reminds me of the tribhangs of Indian Odissi dance also reminds me of my studies in Western classical dance (ballet), experienced in childhood, which, somehow, ended with Paula Ibañez's proposal to seek references from his own history, objects and childhood memories.

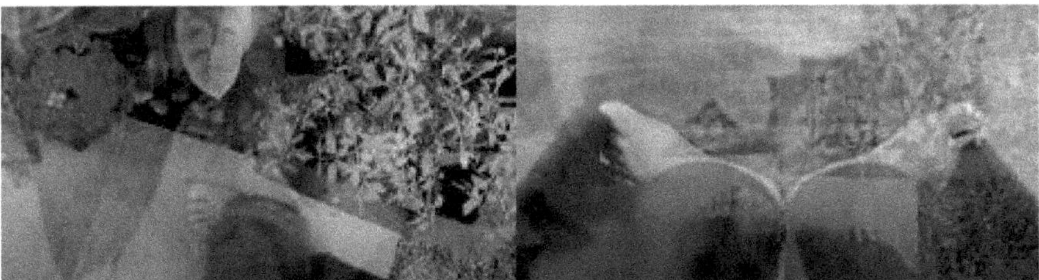

Therefore, in this video, the intercultural perspective is presented in the fact that I rely on images and elements linked to Umbanda – an intercultural religion by its very nature, and because I add movement patterns studied in two different dances to the performance: the ballet, of

European origin, and Odissi dance, of Indian origin. The video was recorded in a single take and later edited.

II. Oxumaré hugs me every morning (Letter 11)

The video performance *Oxumaré hugs me every morning*, like the previous one, also has a reference to Umbanda, but this time to the orixá Oxumaré, linked to the image of the serpent, purple and the idea of ambivalence.

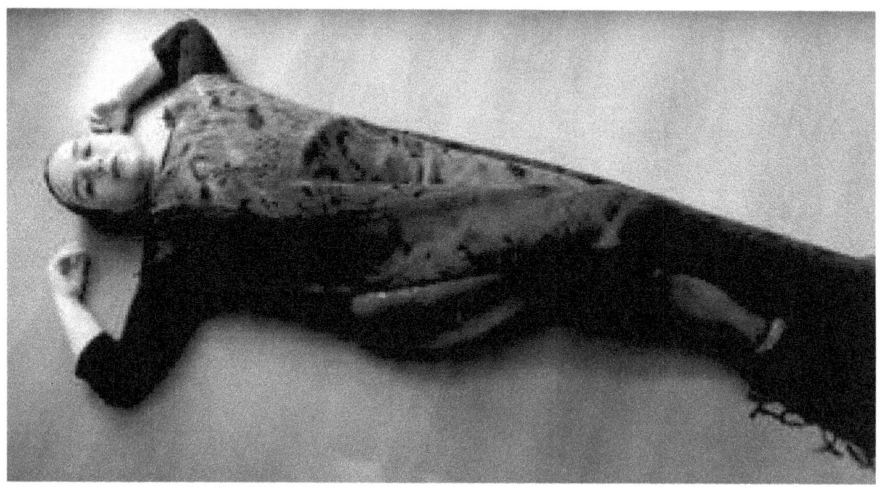

VIDEOPERFORMANCE: https://www.youtube.com/watch?v=UCjBUG-JP0E

I worked with the image of a serpent shedding its skin, a serpent whose skin varied from purple to bluish, a little in reference to the crown chakra and seeking the idea of transcendence, of spirituality.

This video, as well as the following one (Cloud of Powder), was a response to the action proposed by Andrea Albergaria, which was presented in the following format:

Future plans

**Future plans
individuals joined by illusion: courage**

**Old past steps
ancient memories: fear**

**Present looking at the wind
hitting the leaves: dew**

**and the cup of coffee upside down
to be the sludge in the Air: spaces**

**everything is left on one side of the arm:
dust cloud mist
hug (us)**

There was a list of instructions and, in sequence, a poem. The image of the serpent was not in the poem, but in the instructions, when it says: "When recording your experience, listen to the track. There's my voice, the verses. Mentally draw a snake on the ground." As the snake was the strongest image for me, I chose to work with it.

The proposal was simple: also in a single take, I made a meandering sequence on the floor of my son's study room, where a ray of morning sun fell on the floor. In this sequence, I start with the hug, the last verse of the poem – a solitary self-hug of someone who is confined in a small room due to a pandemic. The scarf in shades of purple and blue is superimposed on a contemporary outfit (jeans and a black blouse), glued to the body to purposely highlight the curves of the body that could enhance the image of a curvy serpent.

The sequence is simple and develops by sliding different parts of the body across the floor, occasionally working with fall and recovery studies in American modern dance. I felt the smooth and cold texture of the laminate in a way that took me back to autumn (the time when I recorded the video) and the search for a reference to a milder climate, tending to the cold. This reference made me look for the song Ábrete Corazón, by the Laboratorium Piésni group. I transcribe the lyrics from the Lyricstranslate website[11]:

---

11 https://lyricstranslate.com/pt-br/laboratorium-piesni-abrete-corazon-lyrics.html

Ábrete corazón	Open, heart
Ábrete sentimiento	Open, feeling
Ábrete entendimiento	Open, understanding
Deja a un lado la razón	Put aside reason
Y deja arder el sol	And let the sun burn
Escondido en tu interior	Hidden inside you
Ábrete memoria antigua	Open ancient memory
Escondida	Hidden
En la tierra	On earth
En las plantas	In the plants
Bajo el agua	Underwater
Bajo el fuego	Under fire
Es tiempo ya	It's time now
Ya es hora	It's time
Ábrete corazón	Open, heart
Y recuerda	And remember
Cómo el espíritu cura	how the spirit heals
Cómo el amor sana	how love heals
Cómo el árbol florece y la vida perdura	How the tree blossoms and life endure
Que para llegar a Dios	That to reach God
Hay que aprender a ser humanos	You must learn to be human

The music was chosen to favor the intention of evoking a spiritualist atmosphere linked to ancestry, especially female ancestry, evoked by the power of the harmonies of the singers' voices. In this sense, the filming in plongée is purposeful, which, while placing my female body in a passive position in relation to those who are watching, also allows me to express indifference, untouchability, coldness, and indifference, revealing the strength that the unshakable feminine has when the dynamic femininity quiets herself in her self-sufficiency. A woman's nature is to be independent, and the culture spends all its time trying to make her always complementary (Beauvoir, 2009). I deliberately use, at times, the scarf wrapped around my head like a burqa, as a response to the verse "Y deja arder el sol escondido en tu interior", which translates to "Let the sun burn hidden in your inner" - referring to to the image of the woman who hides either by oppression or, antagonistically, by her own desire.

When editing the video, the sequence was just divided into pieces, without changing the order or overlapping. To intersperse with the pieces, I made recordings of a *tumbergia* tree that I have in front of my house that was in bloom, so that its purple flowers would add to the tones chosen for the video. As in the previous videoperformance, I use movements of my arm passing through the foliage and flowers but, instead of moving like a serpent (and with my hand making mudras as if they were the head of a serpent), I choose to use my hands to caress the leaves. My nails have remnants of the blue paint used in another video performance[12] and I chose to keep them that way, to match the blue of the scarf from the other videodance I had just recorded. I tried to take close-ups of the leaves, so that you can see them in detail and pay attention to aspects that we would ignore in everyday life (such as, for example, the strong yellow tone of the flower's core). I did not avoid the aged flowers because I was interested in showing the cycle of life, like the cycles of a woman who ages/matures.

The male-female ambiguity of Oxumaré is decoded in the different angles through which I try to capture the images of the flowers: sometimes focusing on their center, looking for a similarity with the female reproductive system, sometimes recording their image from the side, to emphasize the phallic aspect. Oxumaré's embrace would be a comfort in a period of global health crisis in which I found myself deprived of exercising my spirituality and which I tried to remedy by resuming all the physical training I knew - from Odissi dance to ballet, from yoga to western contemporary dance, passing through Lian Gong and Chinese martial art, my essential techniques since 2000.

---

12 Lullaby: https://www.youtube.com/watch?v=onASyiDKYzY

III. Cloud of Dust (Letter 15)

For the video "Nuvem de Pó" I started with concrete references from the poem by Andrea Albergaria: starting with the expression "cloud of powder", I pass through the idea of "old memories", the images of "beating the leaves" and the "cup of coffee" and the idea of "reading the dregs in the air".

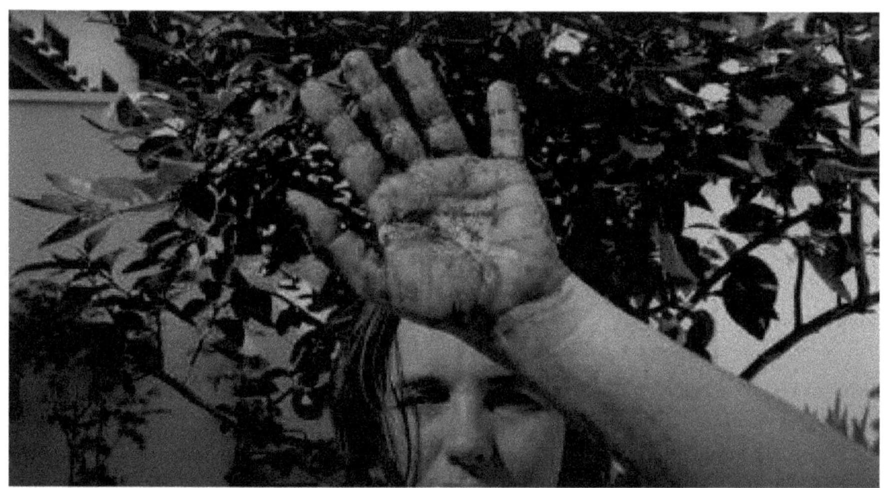

VIDEOPERFORMANCE: https://www.youtube.com/watch?v=p9ep-sAxUW0

They all refer to my childhood lived in the interior of the State of São Paulo, a region in which, in the colonial period, sugar cane and coffee farms were established, and a whole rural culture manifested in the traditions of the viola caipira and dances traditional in the interior of São Paulo. On the negative side, the inhuman legacy of slavery that, until today, is reflected in social inequality and in the occluded political vision of a good part of the middle and upper-middle classes in the interior of São Paulo. On the positive side, the olfactory reminiscent of childhood, easily collapsed by the aroma of coffee that makes up the table of practically every Brazilian.

As in previous videos (and others), opposing the "ancestral" to the contemporary is a topic that is relevant to me, which is why I chose to grind the coffee, for the video, in an electric grinder, even though I have a manual wooder grinder at home too. I chose to record with the lemon tree in the background so that the reference to the bitter aroma of coffee overlapped the reference to the citrus aroma of the lemon. Both are strong, characteristic scents that don't exactly match each other. In the recordings, in addition to the movement sequence with the dregs in my hands, I had also recorded sequences with my feet dirty with earth, but I abandoned those last ones. I tried to focus on the concrete image of "reading the grounds in the air", rubbing the coffee grounds over my hands and on the white clothes I was wearing. Hidden behind the electric grinder (and, later, the strainer), I make some Taijiquan movements with my hands and arms that evoke the same circularity as the grinder's propellers, but in slow motion (more like the cadence of water spiraling down the strainer). The swings of the arms lead me to the spiral of the column. As a result, I say goodbye and drown in coffee.

IV. Healing Waters (Letter 21)

The videoperformance "Águas que curam" was made in response to the action proposed by me to the group, called "Odoyá, Águas que Curam", with editing of a video of mine, some videos by Paula Ibañez and a song by Paula Ibañez.

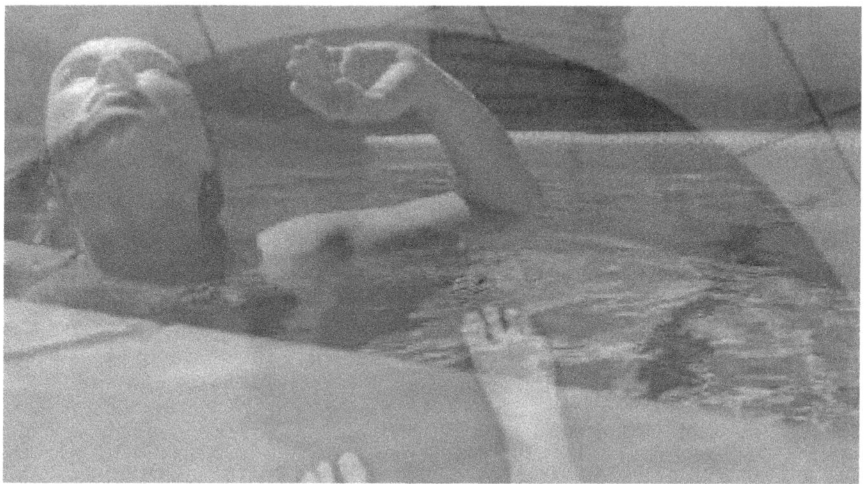

VIDEOPERFORMANCE: https://www.youtube.com/watch?v=sNg-EkBNJJc

They are overlays of images recorded in three different sources of water: swimming pool, faucet, and rain. In the corner, the artist Paula Ibañez uses the echo feature to bring out the malevolent nature of the water and, in the edition, we kept the original sounds of water from our bodies in the interactions (the sound of the body moving the water in the pool, the sound of the water coming out of the faucet and wetting your hands and touching the sink, the sound of rain hitting the floor). I transcribe the lyrics from the "Letras" website[13]:

---

13 https://www.letras.mus.br/socorro-lira/711906/

Senhora Santana ao redor do mundo	Senhora Santana around the world
Aonde ela passava, deixava uma fonte	Where she passed, she left a source
Quando os anjos passam, bebem água dela	When angels pass, drink water from it
Oh que água tão doce, oh senhora tão bela	Oh what a sweet water, oh lady so beautiful
Encontrei Maria na beira do ri	I met Mary on the riverbank
Lavando os paninhos do seu bento fi	Washing her blessed son's clothes
Maria lavava, José estendia	Mary washed, Joseph spread
O menino chorava do fri que sentia	The boy cried from the cold he felt
Os filhos dos homens em berço dourado	The children of men in a golden cradle
E tu, meu menino, em palhas deitado.	And you, my boy, lying on straw.
Calai meu menino, calai meu amor Que a faca que corta não dá tai sem dor	Shut up my boy, shut up my love That the knife that cuts does not cut without pain

The images we evoke also form counterpoints: this time, between the deity woman and the secular woman, who washes clothes, washes her own hands, gets wet in the rain, bathes. Between sacred and profane. In editing, dialogues are created by establishing false sequences between the excerpts, such as when, at minute 1:26, I look completely up (towards the sun) and, in the sequence, Paula is looking down, at the drops of rain hitting the ground. At the end of this excerpt (1:28-1:30) Paula turns the camera and, in the sequence, I turn in the pool with my arms up, in a relatively common movement made by Iemanjá spirits that manifest in *terreiros*.

None of this was planned; we both shot separately in a single take. It was during editing, based on the analysis of the original videos, that these elements that allowed a sequence/dramaturgy to falsify were revealed and

I defined the sequences of the excerpts (there is, therefore – and this is worth noting – a certain amount of "luck").

When Paula washes her head under the tap, for example, along with other elements in the video, this image also evokes something related to Afro-Brazilian spirituality, as the *ori* bath (head bath) is common in these traditions. In editing we also managed to create the illusion, at times, of one of the performers washing the other's head.

We didn't bring the ritual exactly to the scene, but the concept behind it, carried out in other ways and adding to the more global sense of the concept evoked by the video, when we worked with the archetype of Iemanjá, or the Great Mother, like a cloth of sacred background revealed in small everyday gestures of real women.

The images in the videos also allow us to establish a relationship between water, mother, and home, as we have recordings in the environment of a house, interspersed with images in the pool that refer to the idea of rest, rest, relaxation and, in turn, the notion of healing presented in the artistic action proposal. We have, then, the house as a cure, the water as a cure and the mother as a fundamental agent in this process.

V. Dual (Letter 25)

Finally, I briefly comment on the motivations for creating the video *Dual*.

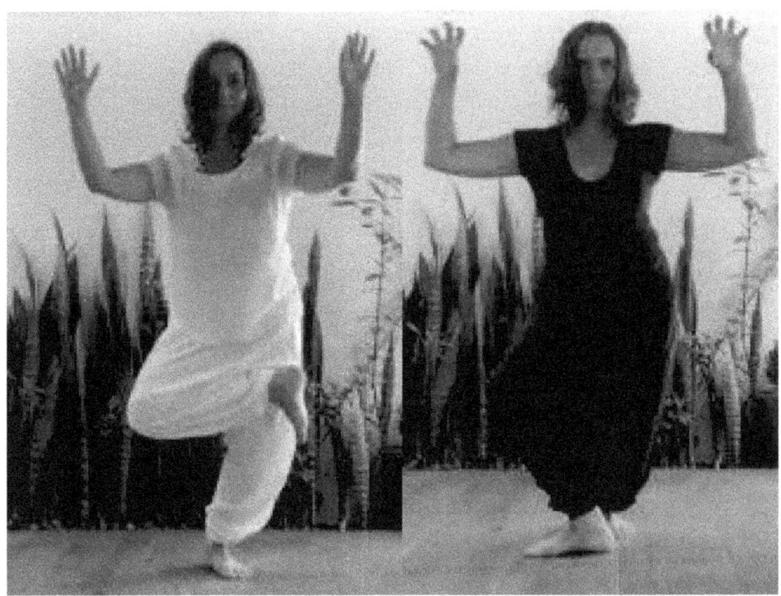

VIDEOPERFORMANCE: https://www.youtube.com/watch?v=4MZB2sStlQI

Responding to Aiswarya's scenic provocation, I created this video, which was also recorded in two takes. My idea was to work on some of the gestures from the Dashavatar choreography, from the Odissi dance repertoire, specifically the part related to Narahsima, due to the dual nature of this character.

I thought of doing two short improvisations: one of them using white clothes and emphasizing aspects such as lightness, serenity or being above worldly matters. In the other, I wore black clothes and tried to emphasize anger, lack of control and the partial view that we humans always have of things.

As I had to use the cell phone in the vertical position to capture the whole body, I came up with the idea of filming the Swords of Saint George from the side corridor of my house (the same ones from Letter 5) in the horizontal position, to superimpose the images of the dance on the plant images. While I was filming the Swords of Saint George I had the idea of shaking the cell phone to use these images in the composition of the version in black clothes. That is: underlying the serene version the Swords of Saint George are stable, and underlying the angry version the Swords of Saint George are shaken.

Just after putting the videos in the editing program, I came up with the idea of using a black and white filter. I didn't do it literally for one and another version of the character, but due to the dynamics of the video – that is, sometimes I use a black and white filter for the calm version and other times for the angry version. I asked Andrea Albergaria to add sound to the video, and only afterwards did I evaluate the overall dynamics of the final video edit and apply the black and white filter to specific sections.

At the time of the creation of this video performance, between June and July 2022, I was experiencing a personal problem that was related to the idea of complementarity between opposite poles in search of balance, positive versus negative, or – if we are to think in the context of Umbanda – the distinctions between what some *terreiros* call right versus left. It would be a way inherent to this specific religion (not necessarily to all religions of African origin) of categorizing some spirits as more connected to the light, to the ethereal, to a more "distant" spirituality, while other spirits would be more connected to matter; in other words. a dualistic perspective.

In the analogy I established with Narahsima, the duality would be linked to the fact that this avatar presents himself as half man, half lion, evidencing, in a certain way, what exists in humans and what differentiates them from other animals – consciousness. Narahsima, however, is a deity linked to destruction and, in the performance, using poetic freedom, in the stretches with white clothes I exaggerated the serenity, to the point that the character in the performance looks more like the avatar Bhuda than with the aspect human of Narahsima. Even so, I chose to stick with Narahsima, assuming poetic freedom and identifying with the image of the lion (simha, singha, simba) which, from the top of the food chain, although strong and potentially murderous, paradoxically expresses the serenity of a being that does not attack gratuitously. That is, the complementarity is not only in the myth linked to this avatar, but in the very nature of the lion animal, as well as in all of us.

In the sound design, Andrea recites a poem of her own in which she lists also polar words – in general, verbs – as the movements announce themselves in the improvised sequence. In the background, the sound of a zither creates a tie that helps to emphasize the complementary character of the two aspects of Narahsima.

Final considerations

The experience of creating videos in partnership with other artists, both Brazilian and Indian ones, has been fruitful as interpretive freedom is always assured to participants. That is, there is the interpretation that I give to the videos I participate in, but other artists participate in these same videos, in different ways, being able to write about other interpretations, based on their personal motivations for creation. I explored this idea in my Associated Professor's thesis, defended in December 2021 (Andraus, 2022), in a topic entitled "Interpretations of author(s) and interpretations of public(s)", in which I argue that there is no problem in having divergences in the personal readings of each author and that, on the contrary, the whole set of possible interpretations for a work, starting with its own authors, makes up the intellectual production derived from a creative process. In this book we find examples of this argument, when we see the same videos being commented, sometimes by different authors. This interpretative richness is ensured by the creative freedom inherent to the symbol, with its character of bearer and synthesis of the unspeakable.

REFERENCES

ANDRAUS, M. B. M. *Cursos d'água, esteiras de vento*: criações de textos e de danças. Curitiba: Editora CRV, 2022.

ANDRAUS, M. B. M. A "outra coisa": ensino de composição artística mediado por vídeo e o uso de tecnologia como estratégia no contexto da pandemia covid-19. *Olhares e Trilhas* (Uberlândia), v. 23, n. 2, abr-jun/2021, pp. 504-518. Disponível em: https://seer.ufu.br/index.php/olharesetrilhas/article/view/60103

BEAUVOIR, S. de. *O segundo sexo*. 2.ed. Trad. Sérgio Milliet. Rio de Janeiro: Nova Fronteira, 2009.

MANZOLLI, J., ANDRAUS, M. B. M. Jardim das Cartas a Presence Ecology: a multimodal and dynamic flow in an installation. *ACM Digital Library*, 2021. Disponível em: https://dl.acm.org/doi/10.1145/3483529.3483680

6

Construction Of The Intangible And Perceiving Sensibilities Through Movement

Aiswarya Lakshmi.G[14]

Using the medium of Bharatanatyam, which is an Indian classical stylised form of dancing, to create sequence patterns for a non-narrative theme is a rather modern and offbeat practice. Bharatanatyam majorly thrives on storytelling and descriptive portrayals. The times it uses abstract dancing is for beautification and aesthetic purposes that adds to the motive of the story being told. Decoding Bharatanatyam movements with the intention of creating an emotional response or expressing an emotion itself is a much less traveled arena. As a trained Bharatanatyam practitioner and researcher, the Intercultural Studies in Performing Arts group provided a space where I could experiment without intense scrutiny on my dance technique and judgment on myself. This allowed me to perceive and create freely.

In performing arts, where the art itself is inseparable from the artist, we are constructing something intangible but yet quite present. To evaluate this art one may need to invite suggestions and feedback. In a healthy community of artists, this practice helps you uncover hidden meanings and perceptions. It is truly a marvel to witness a single dance sequence or such getting multiple interpretations from its viewers. With this forum formed by Dr. K. R. Rajaravivarma and Dr. Mariana Andraus, it also pushed me to open my horizons into the meaning of Bharatanatyam movements I have been practicing for more than half my life. Whether it is the 'Book or Flower' theme (Storytellers: https://youtu.be/GJA2V8a4lSY) proposed by Dr. Mariana or the exploration of space and postures (Light in shadows:

14 Research Scholar, Dept. of Performing Arts, Pondicherry University.

https://youtu.be/fW5hr9SF6Fs), (Quiet: https://youtu.be/JHQ1JPPK_zo) proposed by Dr. Ravivarma, my medium continued to be Bharatanatyam but the sequences that were created could be relatable to a dance researcher in Brazil. Their interpretations of my sequences made sense as I got to open up to formerly unfamiliar sensibilities. A single proposed theme when dealt with Ms. Andrea's understanding of Odissi dance or Dr. Mariana's prowess in Kalaripayattu and western movement technique or Mr. Sumesh's addition of theatrics resulted in varied outcomes, just to mention a few examples.

My proposal, 'Two sides of a coin' was the result of years of Bharatanatayam training where the dancer, while performing a conversational piece (like a Varnam, where pure dance and expression are balanced together in choreography narrating the circumstances of a character or a Padam, where the dancer herself is the character reminiscing or narrating a moment or situation in an expressive piece without the addition of Nritta-pure dance), portrays more than one character on stage assuming the dialogues of the other. In my imagination that dialogue would always be paraphrased when expressed to a third party. This ignited the thought, "what would she/he have said originally?" Even though the crux of the conversation remains the same, in dance, the emotion and the sensibilities can be entirely different from character to character.

Two sides of a coin (Video proposal)

Concept:

Every conversation has more than one version. The differences occur because of the angle of perception of the first person to the second person and the third person and so on.. So far we have explored some abstract ideas on a similar basis. Artists have articulated their versions of such ideas for creating multiple themes.

Proposal:

I propose to explore the two sides of one particular conversation, story, theme, image, metaphor, character, etc., selected by each artist for creating two different versions of the same concept. It could be interpretations of characters in a poem, prose or a conversation between two individuals or two sides of one individual (Dual nature).

Suggestions:

Exploring two sides of a conversation, a story, a character, an inward and outward image of one character, a misunderstanding, a misinterpretation, paraphrasing a friend to his/her lover and so on.

The idea is to focus on human emotions and interpretations; one's suffering could be another's sympathy, one's love could be another's indifference, one's anger could be another's fear, one's joy could be another's jealousy, one's insecurity could be another's anger or one's ability could be another's wonder!

In the forum, the idea was received and delivered with utmost enthusiasm. The proposal was inclusive of any idea or theme by the participants, giving them the opportunity to dive into any performance medium they choose. (I do (not) love (leave) you: https://youtu.be/DTzWItkIWYw), (Ephemeral: https://youtu.be/a1yp2bLHNVY), (Dual: https://youtu.be/4MZB2sStlQI).

As an educated audience, it became an avenue for me to understand varying movement sensibilities when it comes to expression. Regardless of the theme, the artistic intelligence that gets activated inside their mind is deeply rooted in one's cultural and emotional identity. But yet, these sensibilities are still relatable or perceivable to someone outside of the realm even though that specific thought did not seed in them.

During the time of the pandemic, when dance and movement seemed to be practically unrelatable and unachievable, this intercultural forum initiated a healthy community of true artists. As the world is getting more and more advanced, art and artists cannot take a back seat in the name of tradition and practice. Interactions could be elevated with physical proximity. But the forum has successfully formed an interactive and networking space where ideas and thoughts can be bounced off of each other to reach better heights. Along with creating group projects, individual artistry is nourished in these spaces. The possibilities that are created in one's mind by interacting and observing other dancers design their work is one of the best ways to evolve into better artists. Conceptualisations and visualization of artwork becomes effortlessly attainable through exposing oneself to discussions that flow without the barrier of prejudice.

By being part of this forum for Intercultural Studies in Performing Arts group I have learned to let go of inhibitions that restrict my understanding of movement. I believe that perceiving different emotional and cultural sensibilities is the way for an artist to stop their art from being stagnant.

One can continue to only practice their art but can imbibe enormously from multi-cultural exchanges. When constructing the intangible, your perceived sensibilities impart the unique identity that an artist looks for in their every creation. It may seep in without one's knowledge. But, when decoded it will have all the elements that make your art distinct.

7

The Use Of The Aerial Hoop In Video Creations In The Research Group Intercultural Studies In Performing Arts (Letters 4 & 12)

Milena Pereira dos Santos

During social isolation due to the COVID-19 pandemic, the research group Intercultural Studies in Performing Arts developed a series of artistic creations using video as support. These were initiated by proposals in the form of letters, invitations, or poetic provocations from different members of the group, and others who elaborated their answers, sent to the provocateur, who made a video creation based on the responses received. Mariana Andraus and Andrea Albergaria sent me invitations in 2021, which I responded to. I prepared responses that included the aerial hoop, a circus aerial device in a circular format. In this text, I elaborate on how the invitations affected me, the creation of these responses with the hoop, and the use of this circus apparatus with other elements. These video answers were later used as material for the videos "Carta 4 – Entre voos e quedas" and "Carta 12 – Akash"[15].

Mariana Andraus and Andrea Albergaria sent invitations in January and May 2021, respectively. At this time, I was in the second year of my master's degree. I had finished all the courses and was dedicating myself more exclusively to research in progress. My home became where I performed everyday activities, including research and creation. That year, I was already living at the NanoCirco, a cultural venue in Campinas, Brazil, where we work with circus arts and where I learn, teach, and create

---

15 The vídeos are available on Intercultural Studies in Performing Arts YouTube channel.

Carta 4 – Entre voos e quedas: https://www.youtube.com/watch?v=7JTGWD1lAqg

Carta 12 – Akash: https://www.youtube.com/watch?v=ovl0QeuofR0

artistically. It is an open space, full of natural light and plants, and with a structure designed to work with aerial circus equipment[16].

One of the motivations behind choosing to use the aerial hoop was the sense of being able to create with this aerial circus apparatus, one that I have been devoted to for many years since the space was prepared for this purpose. As someone who has worked artistically with aerials and dance, I am interested in using them creatively and associating them with each other. And it is interesting to bring this circus element to the creation of the Intercultural Studies in Performing Arts research group. This is something that identifies me, in a certain way, in the group. I'm the only person working with this art in this context, especially with aerials. By adding more layers of imagery, I can enrich the conversation. Because circus aerials are what I have been most dedicated to in recent years, this is where I have the most creative exploration repertoire.

These are the objective reasons that led me to create using an aerial hoop and dance at NanoCirco. But each of the provocations made by Mariana Andraus and Andrea Albergaria led me to different creative choices with these elements and were intertwined with other ones.

Andrea Albergaria's invitation and the response video "Café" (Coffee)

On May 24, 2021, Andrea sent her provocation-invitation. She sent instructions to guide the creation of material and a poem she wrote:

1. Read the text.

2. Choose a word/expression.

3. Turn this word into a gesture, body, movement, facial expression, or all together. It will be your word.

4. With each stanza, change or, when necessary, use your word.

5. When recording your experience, listen to the track.

There is my voice, the verses. And draw on the floor, mentally, like a serpent. Walk on this path, dancing. Dancing however you like and add your body- word to each space between the stanzas. When you reach the sentence that contains your word, you must stop and stay repeatedly in

---

your movement, in your word, and go back to the beginning or run to the end of the path.

And in the end, dissolve yourself in a cloud, in a mist, in a powder. And hug (me).

Future plans

Individuals joined by illusion: courage

Old past steps

Ancient memories: fear

Present looking at the wind

Hitting the leaves: dew

And the cup of coffee upside down

To be the sludge in the Air: spaces

Everything is left on one side of the arm:

dust cloud mist

hug

This proposal came to me in the final months of my master's degree. While committing to this creation felt like one more thing to do, it was also an opportunity to dance and enjoy creating something outside my master's research. It was an opportunity to delve into Andrea's poem by choosing different elements such as costume, the moment of the day to record (considering that the NanoCirco is an open space), and the movements.

For the response video composition, I chose a flowing red dress for its comfortable texture and fit. I also chose it for the pleasure Andrea's poem suggests. Driven by this sensation, I kept the natural background sound of the NanoCirco, always full of birds, and found places in the space where I stood. The sequence of these pauses moves towards the camera and ends in a moment when I sit on the floor and sunbathe. This is in a moment of stillness and pleasure in the natural heat. Dry cuts were used to make this composition.

Following the instructions, the word I chose was coffee, a drink that I love and that fuels me with energy while comforting me. I even titled coffee my video response. And from that word, I created my own: a wave movement that starts at the belly and travels up to the head and arms, emphasizing the moment of throwing the head upwards.

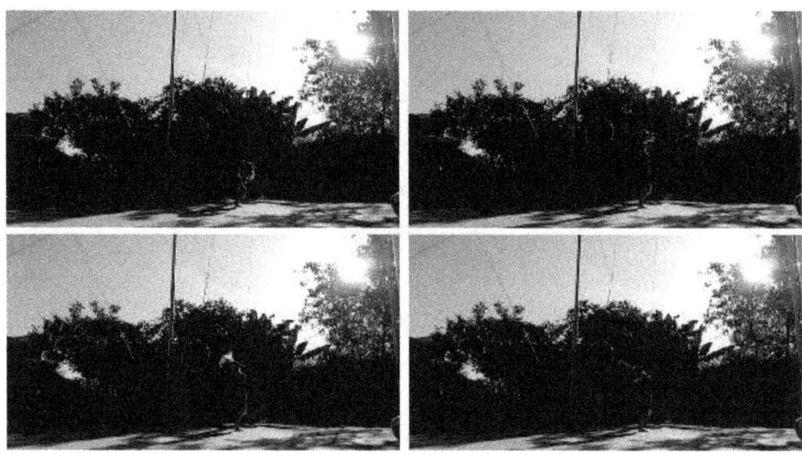

Figure 1. Café screenshots.

My serpentine movement was like a spiral whose center was the aerial hoop. Along this path, I am guided by my arms that open the way for me. Following the instructions, the word-movement is repeated at the end of each stanza. When the voice says coffee, I repeat the movement several times as I spin around myself. I let this combine with the spin, leaning my torso and arms, which leads me towards the embrace.

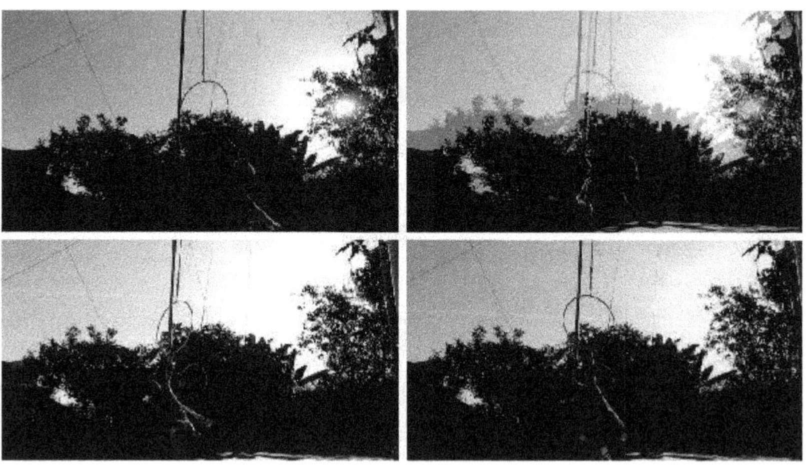

I dilute myself in cloud-mist-dust spinning on the lyre, a movement in which I need to be very focused on myself to perform it with quality and safety, which I also feel embraced for being pleasurable. It's a move I find very beautiful, especially when combined with a flowing costume. It's a hug in video format. As a gift, I offer the beauty I can do to the person who invites me creatively and offers me their beauty.

Café screenshots.

Choosing the aerial hoop allows me this hug-spin that lifts me off the ground, with which I can fly. It adds another layer of movement that is impossible in contact with the floor. In the context of this group, it is something I could offer as an aerialist. For me, it refers to a feeling of embracing myself, that everything culminates and exists in the same body, allying and aligning the perceptions and images of the past, future and present that Andrea's poem evokes: Everything is left on one side of the arm: / dust cloud mist / hug.

Answer to letter #2[17]

On January 12, 2021, Mariana sent her letter to each student under her guidance and other researchers of the group:

- Hello! How long have we not talked? Not so much, isn't it? We always talk to each other, after all :-)

- I am happy with the dialogue we have established for developing your research and consolidating a more collective production pertinent to the intercultural perspective in the performing arts.

- I was curious about everything you did and still do, everything you lived and still lives at the University of Campinas... What makes you want to study interculturality? If you could choose an aspect, a sound, a tone, a cadence of movements that would express the most essential in this encounter with the other, with the different culture, with otherness…

What would that be?

I will ask you for a favor that may seem unusual: that you do not answer this letter with another letter but with a small sequence of movements made by you in your home, using a flower, an apple, or a book. Use your

---

17 Andraus et al, 2022.

cell phone. Don't worry about editing or image resolution... Just use your mobile lying down in a landscape (horizontal) position.

Choose a special outfit for your body. Choose one or more locations in your home. Choose whether to have other people in the video or not. If you want, you can send more than one answer.

The object may be with you on your hands, body, or elsewhere. It can change places, and you can move. The cell phone can move. Table, floor, handrail. Think of your cell phone as an observer who can see you from the front, below, above, and all sides.

Your sequence can be a repetition of the same movement or a chain of movements. It may be a short body-narrated story, or it may not.

Feel free to respond or not to my letter. If you intend to answer, I ask you to do it by 2/12. If you prefer to accept and not manifest soon, everything is fine too. We are in no hurry ... :-)

We were invited to respond to the letter by making a video exploring different movements using a flower, an apple, or a book. We were also invited to explore our motivations for studying interculturality. She suggests ways to use the camera and the object to open exploration possibilities without limiting them.

My first move was to choose one of the three objects to explore, and I quickly decided on the apple. I like the multiplicity of meanings that this fruit carries in different stories: in the relationship between Adam and Eve, in the gift one takes to the teacher (often portrayed in films), the fall of the apple and the understanding of gravity, the popular quote: "One apple a day keeps the doctor away" ... The variety of symbology of the apple made me choose it, but those ideas were not what guided my relationship with it.

Being in the physical space of the circus and recognizing myself as a circus artist, I thought about how to use the apple to connect to this universe. If I had the skill, I would throw knives at the apple. Instead, I associated it with a juggling object. But I am not a juggler either – I barely know how to juggle with three balls – but I had the image of contact juggling in my mind: the movement of sliding and balancing the apple on my body. This is how I began creating: I recorded the first video in which I danced with the apple, especially with my torso, arms, and head close to the camera.

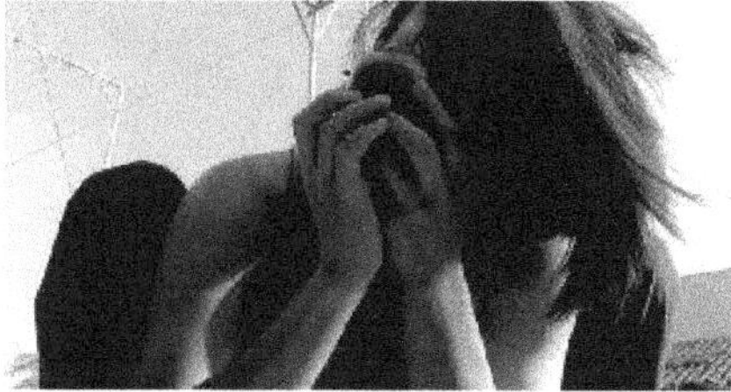 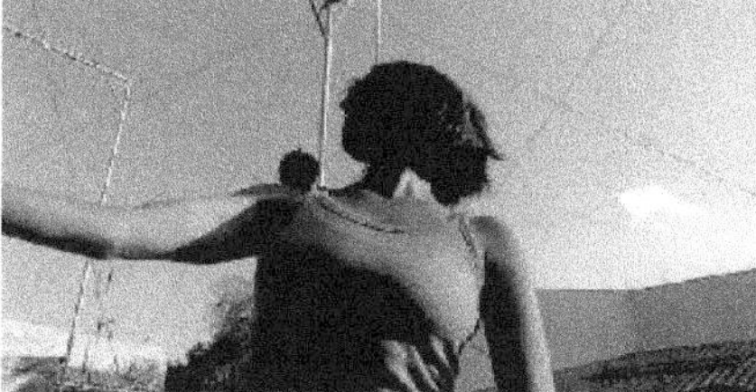

Figure 2. Milena com maçã screenshots.

I balance the apple on my head. I try to walk, turn, and spin without dropping the apple while walking towards the aerial hoop, hanging in space and ready for use. I started a few attempts to climb up and move on the hoop while keeping the apple balanced on my head. This was a difficult task. I managed to perform some postures, but the fall happened many times. Since gravity didn't stop acting and my skill wasn't so great to keep the fruit-object over my head, I decided to incorporate this event and explore my reaction when the apple hit the ground: I would watch the fall happen, do something that wasn't possible while balancing the apple (being upside down, for example), and go to the ground. These actions were recorded from different angles and at different times of the day, generating distinct video images.

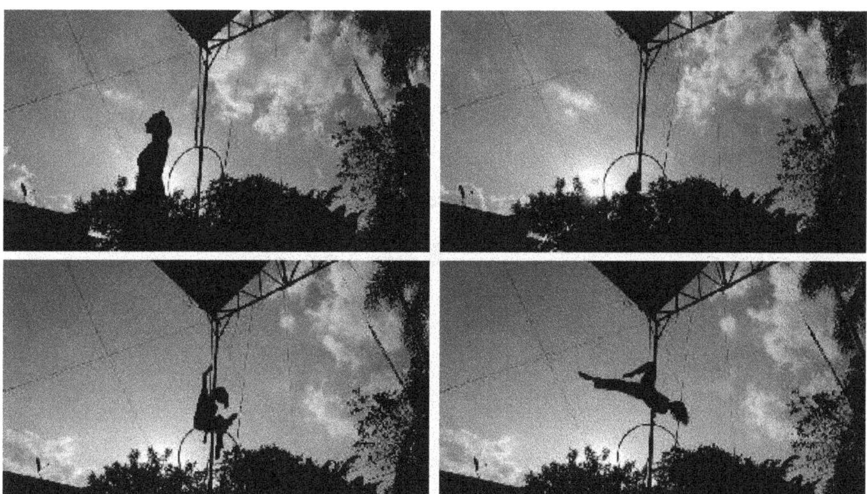

Figure 3. Milena na lira contra luz screenshots.

Another inspiration for the actions in the hoop was the birds in NanoCirco: their perching and permanence. It would be interesting to incorporate them into the dance. I recorded two birds perched on a steel cable: one arrived first, then another landed and approached, interacted a bit and left. Perching and permanence inspired me, and I wanted to reproduce them.

The hoop would be my ally at that moment, the apparatus on which I would be a bird and with which I also artistically recognize myself. For me, this part of the exploration answers the question: "What makes you want to study interculturality? If you could choose an aspect, a sound, a tone, a cadence of movements that would express the most essential in this encounter with the other, with the different culture, with otherness... What would that be?"

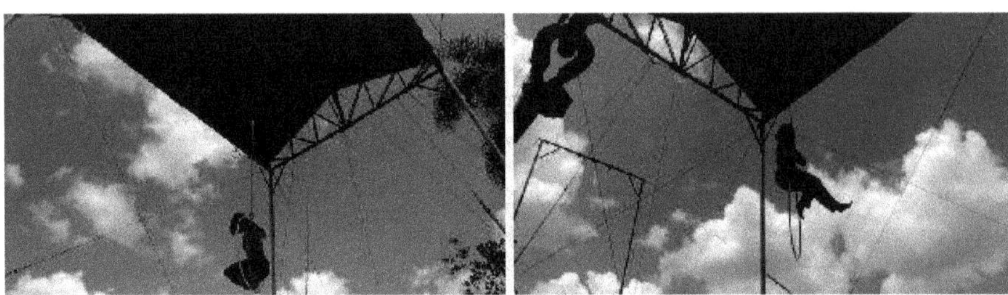

Milena na lira screenshots.

Since video creation was unfamiliar to me, I had to navigate through moments of trying it out without the camera. I recorded, watched, understood what could be different, and recorded again. The process of recording, watching, and re-recording occurred a few times to test angles, shots, light, etc. With no intention of developing a narrative sense for my actions, I wanted to create stimulating and possibly beautiful images for the video, with a subtle touch of the impressive circus universe around me. These were my choices to answer Mariana about what interests me in interculturality.

This response letter was one of the materials for "Carta 4 – Entre voos e quedas". The creation of this video was covered in the article "Letter #5: Reflections on perception-action in the creative process of "Entre voos e quedas" (Andraus et al, 2022).

Final considerations

My choice to work with the aerial hoop in both creations is a result of my close relationship with the circus discipline, my technical mastery, and my artistic interest in it. For the answers, in addition to performing with this apparatus, I elaborate on how other elements compose the movement, the scene, and the images. The hoop becomes a starting point for connections with other elements, supporting the creative process based on movement exploration and imagery composition for video. For Andrea's proposal, I created an association of movement in which the hoop provides me with pleasurable action and synthesis. This is a knot between the present, past, and future, a hug. In replying to Mariana's letter, I associate the balance of an apple on my head while I move on the hoop and the image of perching and remaining inspired by the birds.

Resuming these creative processes aiming to report and observe how they happened for me, the pathways I walked by and how I chose the movements and compositions made me return to the questions proposed by the provocateurs. It is not merely an assumption that I am a circus artist, but rather a desire to create with the aerial hoop, an aerial apparatus I decided to dedicate myself to several years ago. Once I recognize myself as a circus artist, I relate to many others with knowledge of this field. And from this perspective, I see my interest in investigating interculturality in the performing arts: from the places where I recognize myself artistically.

References

ANDRAUS, M. B. M., MANZOLLI, J., SANTOS, M. P. Letter #5: Reflexions on perception-action in the creative process of Entre voos e quedas. **Journal of Music and Dance**, v. 12, n. 1, jul-dez/2022, pp. 1-10. Disponível em:

https://academicjournals.org/journal/JMD/article-abstract/603BB1A69980

8

Dance To My Deaths (Letter 10)

Flávia Pagliusi[18]

On that day, I had chosen some colored threads to embroider a skirt. Not because I knew how to do it, but because I felt the need to watch the tread crossing the waves of the fabric, joining one piece to the other. For some unknown reason, that movement was reassuring.

Putting the parts together.

I didn't know it yet, but shortly I was going to experience my death. To inattentive ears, perhaps these words might abuse the superlative, but this is the deception that a shallow look can lead to. Yes, that day I died. I said goodbye to a past lived in prose and vivid in simple verses, cacophonous in the end, undeniable, but full of what only the heart can overflow. I got rid of the last tendrils that I was insisting to extend in space, when I was trying to embody what was already a memory. And as I desperately threw myself into the finitude that only death seems to fit, I felt myself free. Surprisingly freed from what was already putrid in me, but which I kept carrying in an empty suitcase. It was from my flesh lying among worms and pasture that I was reborn in me.

Through the high point of the COVID-19 pandemic in 2021, we from the Unicamp Intercultural Studies in Performing Arts research group were looking for ways to continue creating and dancing. In this research, the videos, crudely recorded through our cell phone cameras, began to capture movements in the intimate spaces of our homes, a creative choice, but also a political one, given the Brazilian context at the time. In one of those days of stagnation and anxiety, I received a provocation from Professor Mariana Baruco, advisor, and master in the ways of academic and personal life,

---

18 Bachelor in Dance, Master in Performing Arts and PhD student in Performing Arts at the University of Campinas, psychoanalyst and art therapy.

suggesting that we choose three objects to dance with. The experience should be recorded and sent to her.

After receiving these guidelines and reflecting for a moment, my dancing partners were selected: a dress, a sewing machine and a handful of dry leaves collected on a square's ground. The first two sprang up as if giving form to my mother's memory.

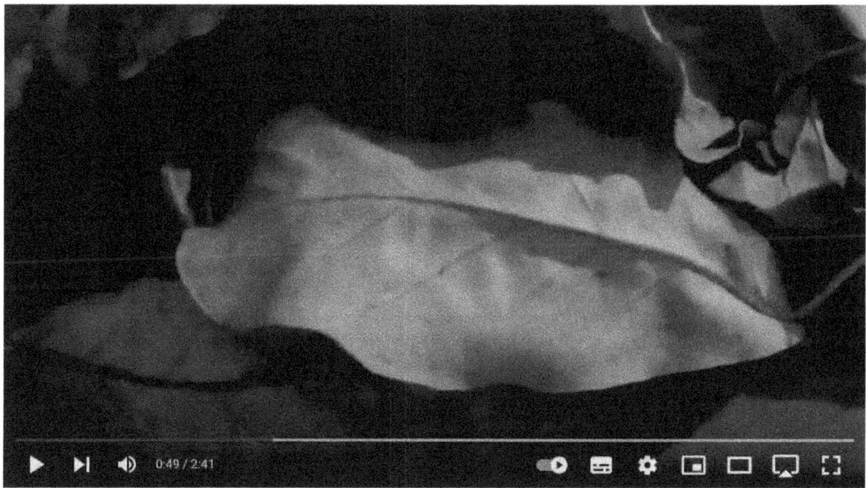

Made of white lacy fabric, decorated with colorful flowers and small sparkling stones, the dress, probably bought by her at a handicraft fair during a family trip to the north coast of São Paulo, had been hanging empty in my wardrobe for years. Even in its melancholy, the piece of clothing exuded a spring air that matched my mother's fresh personality. A little further up, tucked away in a corner of the same cabinet and wrapped in plastic, resting silently and yellowed by the years, her old sewing machine. Countless times I saw her pressing the pedal and making the needle go up and down hurriedly in the contraption's mechanism, always a great mystery to me. I could never figure out the threads' ways through the many levers, holes, and pulleys. The noise of the acceleration, the amber light emitted by the machine and, above all, the smell that insisted on releasing from its gears brought back memories from afar.

As for the leaves, they came from a conversation with Professor Baruco which I honestly don't remember very well. It's possible that we talked for hours standing on a sidewalk in the sun while pretending to say goodbye, only to keep talking a bit longer. Maybe we were talking about my anxieties and creative fears, a recurrent theme at that time, and the dry leaves appeared. They showed up and I liked it. Some time later, on any given day, armed with a plastic bag and some friendly hands that agreed to help me with the task, I went to a square and came back loaded with dry leaves and the desire to dance.

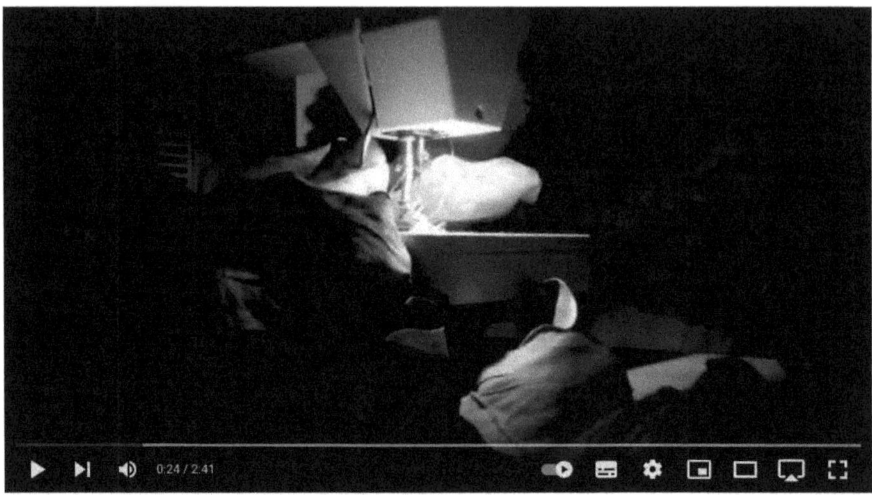

First, I threw the plants on the living room floor of the small apartment where I lived and felt the contact of the soles of my feet with that curdled surface covered in what no longer was. The sound of crunching underfoot made music for motion research. Meanwhile, both the dress and the sewing machine watched me from the wooden table. I realized that it was easier to start with the leaves, for it would take courage to assume those objects that now, at least in theory, were mine, but that persisted in frightening fantasies.

I decided to get the dress. Immediately, a series of images, sensations and feelings invaded my body. Memories of truth and fiction passed quickly, carrying the hollow weight of mourning. The empty dress denounced the missing body, giving form to absence and laying lifeless in my hands. *Saudade* made of fabric. Stealing Hijikata's words (Baiocchi, 1992, p. 55, our translation), "As a little child, I thought [...] that form appears because it disappears. That its disappearance shows its form even more clearly". Gradually, however, with time and patience, I began to move with it close to my skin, as if inviting it to a dance. I sharpened my perceptions, attentive to the concrete information that the dress gave me: its weight, its smell, its textures. What more could that piece of clothing tell me besides what I already knew? And I wore it on the outside, getting used to the idea of occupying that empty space without, however, being swallowed up by it. As it danced in small movements, I experienced longing. Losing myself, doubting the future, feeling immense pain without knowing its genesis. Walking with clouded eyes, being afraid of the next step, even knowing that it is inevitable. The fear that memories would be swallowed up by time, the fear of forgetting. Holding water with my hands, drying rivers with pieces of cleaning clothes.

When I finally put it on for the first time, I looked at myself in the mirror as if assimilating my own image after a long time. Yes, I was still myself! I risked a few movements starting with my feet, which no longer wanted to go back to the dry leaves. Guided by them, I stepped and thread and trampled on paths, knowing the ways though my feet. Gradually, a continuum of circular movements and smooth turns was drawn; fingers always open, seeking to embrace the whole floor, feeling it.

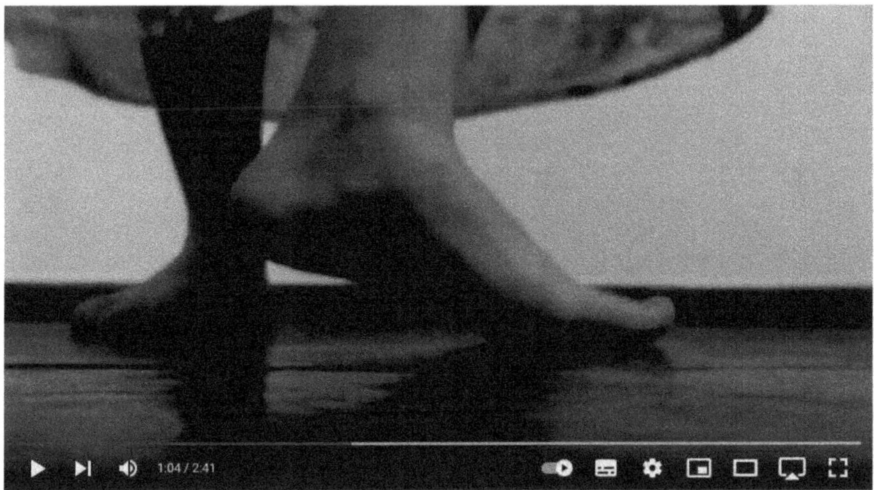

"When you walk, be careful. You might be walking over the dead", said Ohno (BAIOCCHI, 1995, p. 44, our translation). The firm surface, the safe ground that anchors the flourishing strengthening the roots also gives shelter to the worms that, in death, devour. It is womb and it is tomb. Still echoing the butoh master's words, "We exist today thanks to the accumulation of countless deaths... I am the summary of a series of deaths accumulated within me" (BAIOCCHI, 1995, p. 43, our translation). In the simplicity of my dance, I faced the cruelty, in the sense given by Antonin Artaud, of Ohno's lines. From the invisible threads I wove on my mother's sewing machine, which I never knew how to use, I was lining up my deaths on dry leaves.

We are dying. Every day. So dying wouldn't be living?

Then, I suddenly realized that "Alinhavos" is a dance of death. Of my mother's death, but also of the daughter I was. Of the body, but also of childhood. Of each leaf that, in the fulfillment of its own time, detaches itself from the tree and dries up, but also of what is reborn from the sewing of all these lived times. It's about dealing with the brevity and finitude of things, with powerlessness and smallness. It is, ultimately, a confirmation of the castration to which we are all subjected. But at the same time, it is also a dance of life. Life that resurfaces from the possibilities suggested by the stitching together of the memory traces that constitute us.

On that day, I lived my death. And I dare say that it was well lived.

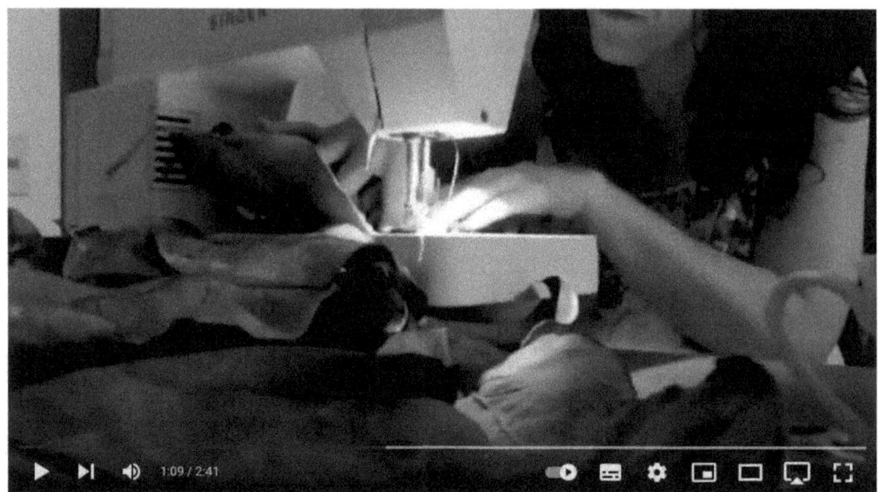

REFERENCES

BAIOCCHI, Maura. *Butoh:* dança veredas d'alma. São Paulo: Palas Athena, 1995.

9

Diasporic Transmutations In Water: From Dance To Cosmos (Letter 22)

Jonatas Lopes de Matos Santos[19]

Like many martial artists, I am provoked by the famous speech of Bruce Lee, in an interview with Pierre Berton:

Empty your mind, be formless, shapeless - like water. Now you put water into a cup, it becomes the cup, you put water into a bottle, it becomes the bottle, you put it in a teapot, it becomes the teapot. Now water can flow or it can crash. Be water, my friend (LEE, 1971).

And, like many Bahian Brazilians, I am honored to also dance, blessed by the tranquility and loveliness of Odoyá, in the happy synchronicity of writing very close to the date of his homage, one of the most beautiful festivals in Salvador, the 2nd of February.

Filled with digressions, the provocation "Waters that heal" left me between juxtapositions of ancestry and precious wisdom. The creative motto of the incursion into dance "Carta 22 - Fios d'água" led me to two reflexive directions: quality of movement in function of water behaviors and identity activations from the verb to heal ("curar" in Portuguese).

---

19 I'm from Bahia, from the railway suburb of Salvador, a martial and dance artist, who researches the relationship between dance, martiality, traditional knowledge and pop culture. Master's student in dance and specialist in art education at UFBA. Graduated in the martial art of Hapkido and, currently, I work as a Dojang instructor and self-defense advisor. Massage therapist specializing in treatment related to body tension due to postural or somatized issues.

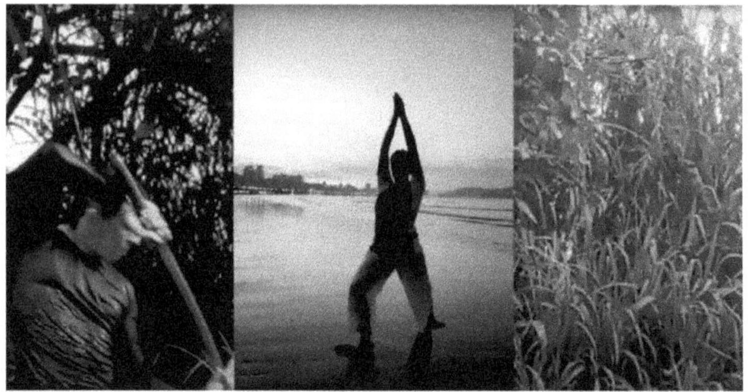

VIDEOPERFORMANCE: https://www.youtube.com/watch?v=F_b73ORsHbs

Activating adaptability, as it is quite useful for optimizing combat solutions, is often referred to in seminars and martial arts classes. The fight is an environment of concurrent and constant changes, which is related to the main qualities that water brings. I tend to believe that part of the martial arts traditions, especially the ones I am part of, pursue movement research aligned with qualities such as stability, strength, balance, rigor, calm and solidity. These qualities are related to the way the mountain is defined, in the I Ching[20]. Seeking to better understand how this alchemical process works, the challenge of being a martial artist, who acts like water, is how to transmute mountain (Gen) into water (Kan), a true transformation of nature. According to the I Ching (2016), the mountain trigram is symbolized by a yang being raised by two yin:

Picture 01 - hexagram symbolizing the mountain (艮 gèn).

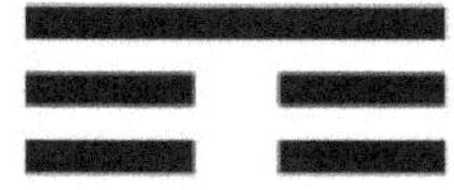

Fonte: I CHING: O Livro das Mutações (2016).

Já a água é simbolizada por trigrama como um yang entre dois yin:

Picture 02 - hexagram symbolizing the water (坎 kǎn).

---

20 The I Ching or The Book of Changes is one of the main works of traditional Chinese thought. Sometimes used as a philosophical treatise, reflecting on the symbolic movements of the elements of nature, sometimes used as an oracular method (I CHING: O Livro das Mutações, 2006).

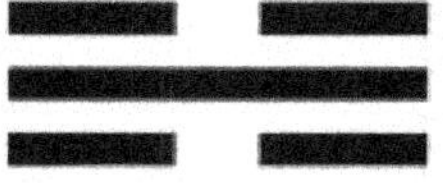

Fonte: I CHING: O Livro das Mutações (2016).

The descent of yang from the top to the middle is to change the structures of how propositional principles (yang) and receptive principles (yin) move. The submergence of yang and the emergence of yin are involved with this dance in tentative and poetic martiality. Dance-transmutation has been my profession, but I will end by insisting on the metaphor of the mountain also because of the imaginary of samurai masters and Shaolin abbots who, in order to develop their mastery, isolated themselves in mountains and assimilated their properties. By sword, by blows, by base, by repertoire, my dance was motivated by this outpouring, this type of movement of the waters, starting from the mountain. So, the performative paths of going up and down, crystallizing and dissolving, were searches inspired by this alchemical perspective. In the *Tao Te Jing[21]*, there is a poem that presents water as a metaphor for transformation, endowed with the power to overcome changing conditions, the poem 78:

[...]
Nothing is smoother and softer than water
However, to attack what is rigid and hard
Nothing can get ahead of her
nothing can replace it
Like this
Softness beats strength
Soft beats hard
under the sky
There is no one who does not know
There is no one who can practice it
[...]
(TSE, 2016, p.81)

---

21 Tao Te Ching, Dao de Jing or Tao te king (Chinese: 道德經, Dàodé jīng), commonly translated as The Book of the Way and Virtue, is one of the treatises on traditional Chinese thought. Main reference of Taoism, through poems, establishes the spirit of the Taoist perspective. It was written between 350 and 250 BC Its authorship is traditionally attributed to Lao Tzi (literally, "Old Master") (TSE, 2016).

Although we are dancing here between fights and philosophies, Taoist and Zen Buddhist religious sermons explore how transcendence is taught through the behavior of nature's elements. Not just for combat solutions, part of Lao Tzu's concern involves how to govern himself and the nation. Therefore, water teaches the principles of yin-yang, and assimilating ourselves to it contributes to self-development. So, in the wake of how water is versatile, in studies of the body in martiality, the reference is clear in a dialogical relationship, you adapt to a blow or maneuver. However, this artistic endeavor was a duet resulting from two solos. And part of my dive turned to a performative perspective of spillage, reflecting the power that my memory brought me about the behavior of waves. I point out that the contours of my memory may have specific types of waves, because, grown in the sands and waters of the railroad suburb of Salvador[22], the waves on the beaches are the smoothest in Baía de Todos os Santos, frustration of any surfer, relief of fishermen and mothers of young children.So, along with the water that settled into the glass in my hand, I poured it out. And, synchronically with the title, with the blunt edge of my sword, I poured an edge of water divided over me.

The verb cure[23], in Portuguese, which, between poetry and irony, has two distinct semantic fields: action to restore health; and dry in smoke, sun or fresh air. Summoned to me a dance with the provocation about healing waters brings a first logical relationship, the waters tend to heal. Washing wounds, cooling inflammation, relaxing tensions, de-stressing exploited workers, it really seems that the waters, in addition to being the mother of the Rio Vermelho[24], perhaps she is also the mother of all pharmacies. Curing is also a process prior to the use of refrigerators to preserve food, through dehydration of meat. And, a descendant of street vendors and ranchers from the Bahian countryside, in the horizons of my ancestry, there is this perspective, dryness as both a problem and a solution. Part of my healing agenda (both ways) from my childhood was the season in my relatives' gardens on my mother's side. In the villages of Salgadália, Santa Rosa and Laginha (on the borders of Conceição de Coité - BA and Retirolândia - BA, region of the agreste region of Bahia), it was common

---

22 The Subúrbio Ferroviário de Salvador is the name given to the set of neighborhoods on the borders of Salvador towards the innermost part of Baía de Todos os Santos (the bay where the city of Salvador is located). It is a peripheral region of Salvador known for the railway line that connects the neighborhood of Calçada, which is in the region known as Cidade Baixa (downtown), to the suburban neighborhood of Paripe, which is in the northwest region of Salvador, known for being the penultimate neighborhood from Salvador in this region.

23 "Curar" verb. Consulted in the Michaelis Dictionary of the Portuguese Language. Available at https://michaelis.uol.com.br/moderno-portugues/busca/portugues-brasileiro/curar/. Accessed on 11 Jan 2023.

24 Neighborhood of Salvador where festivities take place in honor of Odoyá, Iemanjá.

to see, like clothes hanging out, fresh meat in the process of becoming backcountry meat (the process of cure). How can there be so much water and so much dryness in the same state, seashells in the water and dried snail shells on rocks, would they be blessed by Odoyá equally? Not only when Antônio Conselheiro's[25] prophecy that "the waste will turn into the sea", Odoyá reaches his children even far away. However, among my personal rites, I have already washed waste shells in my seas, as a personal coherence. So, part of the work's motivating drive, there is water in scarcity, and, in breaths of movement, I walk a path from liquidity to healing (drying to preserve, but also to recover the health of the spirit).

To crown the immersion in these waters and cures, assuming the diasporic nature (African and Asian) of this incursion, I dress referencing yin-yang and in nagô braid. In the direction of what has been how I have been recognized in the world, this choice of clothing has to do with two movements that I have been assuming: acceptance of the ancestries that constitute me and the reverence of the ancestries that were presented to me.

The first movement concerns the result of numerous political struggles of race awareness in a racist scenario in which Brazil is inserted. I have recognized myself as a light-skinned black subject (often recognized as pardo), immersed in a peripheral Bahian culture, which is made up of diasporic black cultures. Shissai Chozan[26] and Takuan Soho[27] comment on the best state of mind that the martial artist should have, which is the *fudochi*, the immobile mind. The main metaphor, used to illustrate what *fudochi* is, is the image of a boat that remains motionless, but moves through the waters. But this motionless mobility, metaphorized by a boat passing through the waters, departs from the seas of my horizons, from Baía de Todos os Santos. Growing up in seas full of offerings to Odoyá, to be a potent martial artist, he would be blessed by the queen of waters, just before the goddess Kannon[28], samurai goddess.

---

25 Antônio Vicente Mendes Maciel (Nova Vila de Campo Maior, March 13, 1830 – Canudos, September 22, 1897), better known as Antônio Conselheiro, also calling himself "the pilgrim". A charismatic figure, he acquired a messianic dimension when he led the Canudos camp, a small village in the backlands of Bahia (FRAZÃO, 2022).

26 Shissai Chozan was a samurai of unknown biography who lived in the Kyoho era (1716-35) in Osaka, where he was a very active writer. He studied Japanese and Chinese thought; with particular preference for the Chinese Taoists Lao Tzu and Chuang Zu. He wrote Tengu-geijutsu-ron, a work that appears in several collections dealing with philosophy and martial arts (KAMMER, 2010).

27Takuan Soho was a Buddhist monk (December 24, 1573 - January 27, 1645) who wrote about Zen Buddhism in the contexts of Tokugawa period Japan, which involved the appreciation and complexification of the warrior's path.

28Kannon Bosatsu (romanization from Japanese) is the Deity of Compassion and Mercy worshiped by Buddhists.

The second movement deals with my immersion in Chinese, Japanese and Korean philosophical perspectives, which sometimes takes principles for movement studies in dance and fighting, sometimes uses principles for the development of poetic contextual constructions. Perspectives that relate to traditions currently known as Taoist, Buddhist, Shintoist and Confucianist, who had in martial arts spaces of symbolic work laboratories, have been ancestors that, honorably, I have been presented between serendipities and studies.

However, I brought these roots, which at times gave me life, at other times revitalized me by grafting, into the preparation of this work. I commented on how the idea of water and healing hit me, so I tried to experiment with some qualities of movement: how to move with stability, readiness and variation while holding a glass of water; accurate sword strikes with fluid recovery; and continuous movements without alteration when hit by running water. I tried combined sword solutions balancing a glass of water on the wire, however, the dances found decant more for sustaining the materiality of the body than the senses of cure and water.

A glass of water, in a sense, is a glass of revitalization for a healed (parched) body. However, moving with stability and variation protecting a body of water called me to liquid and spiral qualities, as pauses without deceleration would lead the water to continue moving, according to the principle of inertia.

It is part of the agenda of my dance and martial arts research, movement solutions with the collaboration of extensions such as swords and sticks. When I propose to dance with a sword, I try to open possibilities of movements, because, among the martial arts repertoires, the action of striking is predominant, and, in a certain way, it takes all performativity due to the movement that ends very quickly, among the repertoires I know. In this endeavor, what motivated me was the movement of the waters in changing relief, like rivers in mountain relief, which with the sword I traversed waterfalls and flooding.

Finally, among the procedural regimes, I had the search for continuity even affected by water. Inspired by the estuary (the river flows into the sea) and the tributary (the river flows into another river), as movement paths, they bring different qualities of moving when being hit by the water. Getting wet brings performance to the water itself, modifying the texture of the hair, the shine of the skin, modifying the fit of the clothes and acquiring other paths from other spills. There is a subtle imagery quality to the presence of the wet sword, for its refractory quality is common with water, and at times the sword and water's threads intermingle, and I am pleased to see that, in some measure, I am extended pouring.

The emergence of video work brought a veritable meeting of diasporic waters. Honorably, I met with Drica Ribeiro in this work, which invoked other waters. Taking root in front of the territories of Oyá (with horizons that rhyme with mine), Drica brought the calm and soul of the Indian ceremony that greeted our waters. Our differences in rhythm, differences in flow and movement between planes are the very materiality of differences between tides and seas. In conversation with Mariana Andraus about the title given to the edition, she commented on the chosen pun: the word 'fio", in Portuguese, means thread, but it is also an oral and colloquial form, in some regions of the country, for the word "filho" (son). So, in addition to water streams, the video performance could also refer to "sons of water", in reference to the Afro-Brazilian deity Iemanjá. We would be the two performers on the scene, therefore, children of the water (one in the sea and the other in the waterfall).

Faced with the conception and editing script by Mariana Andraus and set to music by Drica Ribeiro, I am grateful for the opportunity to once again move under the umbrella of my personal prayer: "I am a creek where the ocean flows".

Partnership - Enchantments in meetings: diasporas of Self and Horizons in 29 Letters

In the midst of diasporas of affections and diasporas of aesthetics, we engage in 29 dance-letters, we dance looking inward and looking at our horizons. I feel that in this space of experimentation we could see how the diasporic movement of expressiveness has been found. This diaspora has several orders, mainly expanding the perspective of what is dispersive. As letters, we have taken amalgamations of cosmoreflexive processes to other territories, both geographic and knowledge. We had movements that dispersed from their orthodoxies, they found each other: music, traditional dances, circus, martial arts, theater; arts and ways of life were tracing new orders of sender-letter-recipient within these poetics. I do not include the specific dimensions of the technological poetics of this process because the 29 letters were immersed in this sea, some deeper, others more on the surface. We find potential both in the way we connect intimacies, when we connect holistic perspectives of the universes we participate in. We had moving imagery: an aphrodiasporic goddess appreciating the seas of India; the same sky appreciating dances closer or less close to it; among so many powers. Linked by the invitation to interact, they demonstrate that there is pulsating life in the diaspora.

REFERENCES

FRAZÃO, Dilva. **Antônio Conselheiro**: Brazilian social and religious leader. E-Biography. 2022. Available at: https://www.ebiografia.com/antonio_conselheiro/. Accessed on: 23 Feb. 2023.

I CHING: **O Livro das Mutações**. Richard Wilhelm translation. 1 ed. São Paulo: Pensamento, 2006. 546 p. Translation of: I Ching.

KAMMER, Reinhard. **Zen in the art of wielding the sword**: the ancient Japanese art of fencing. Translation Alayde Mutzenbecher. 13. ed. São Paulo: Editora Pensamento, 2010. 112 p. Translation of: Die Kunst das Schwert zu Führen. This book contains the core of Shissai Chozan's work Tengu-geijutsu-ron (17th century).

Lee, Bruce. Interview on Pierre Berton Show – **The Mandarin Superstar** – given December 9, 1971. Available at: dailymotion.com/video/x29c8ez. Access 07 Oct. 2020.

SOHO, Takuan. **The Mysterious Records of the Still Mind**. Translation Eric Michael Shahan (English); Leandro Diaz Napolitano (Portuguese). 1 ed. Tokyo: Eric Michael Shahan, 2020. 106 p. Translation of: 不動智神妙録 (Fudochi Shimmyo Roku).

TSE, Lao. **Tao Te Ching**. Translation Wu Juh Cherng. s.l: Sociedade Taoísta do Brasil, 2016. Translation of: 道德經, Dàodé jīng. Available at: http://www.dominiopublico.gov.br/download/texto/le000004.pdf. Accessed on: 24 Jan. 2023.

10

An Experience Report Of The Videos You Created Yourself: Concepts, Approaches, Method, Tools, Forms, Creative Process, Rehearsal System (Letters 18, 22 & 28)

Adriana Suely Queiroz Ribeiro

The videos produced by me during the period 2020 to 2022 for the Intercultural Studies in Performing Arts group had as their concept the exploration of outdoor spaces. In my view, internal spaces, everyday environments such as the bedroom, the house, family relationships have become very saturated to the point of almost causing a short circuit in these interactions. Even so, these internal spaces were explored in order to find expanded perceptions on how to live with us, with our pain, fears and anxieties and other not so comfortable feelings that surfaced during the pandemic period. Our work as artists was to transit through these fields of struggle and internal resistance to make our art sprout even in small or almost non-existent spaces within our homes.

As soon as it was possible to leave the house after the lockdown, exploring other environments outside the spaces of our homes, it seemed the most natural thing to do. The approaches that used in this study were the body in communication with the spaces (internal and external) to create performative arrangements. Between is the discrete word that runs through the notes that follow. Like a crest line between two chasms – this secret region above which Jean Genet (2000, p. 39) tells us, this solitude where beings and things take refuge, and which configures an "unassailable singularity.

The performances that developed in the spaces contained many elements, such as landscape, animals, plants, human bodies, the sea, the clouds, and the sky. But the element of the interval, the Ma, a particularly japanese notion that helps us to understand these empty spaces that are pure possibility: minimal existences, close to nothing and perfectly unfinished, whose proper rest (the art that specifies and legitimizes them) is to elicit other gestures, other expressions, and other fractions of reality.

Water leaves performance- Letter 18

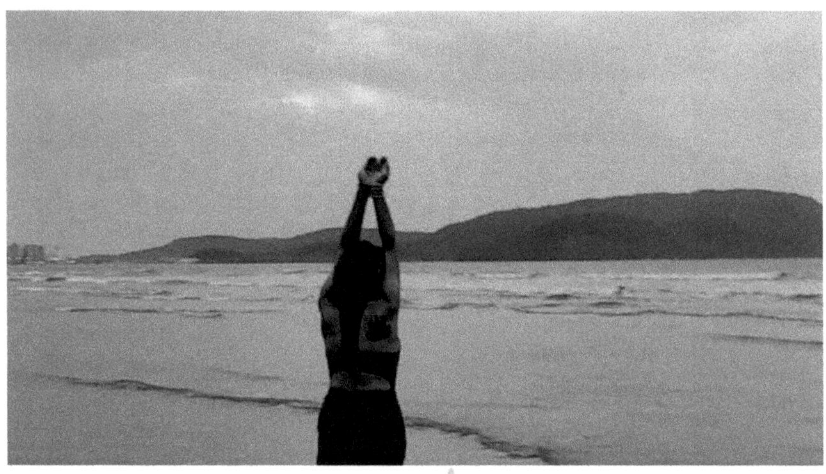

VIDEOPERFORMANCE: https://www.youtube.com/watch?v=_Ia44GvAX_I

How does a leaf that falls into water behave? She is left to the whim of the wind and the flow of water and is simply carried away by this movement. My intention in this performance was to translate this feeling. During the pandemic period we could feel how necessary this surrender to cosmic forces was. The leaves that fall from the trees and then into the water are the substrate of life on earth. As i am from the Amazon, realize how much life and abundance there can be in the leaves that hover in the waters of the forest or even the sea. They decompose and serve as a substrate for soil and other plants. The pandemic context has brought us to reflect on how we have been dirtying and staining our waters, our soil and all other living organisms (including ourselves). Bringing this reflection through the performing arts makes me very happy.

On the recording of the performance Folhas d'água, I recorded the video on a beach in the city of Santos, on the coast of São Paulo. On many occasions, my laboratory for this performance was to pick a leaf or a flower and offer it to Iemanjá, who in Brazilian culture represents the Universal Mother, the mother of the sea whose children are both fish and human beings. Observing the flow of water leaves and the silent presence of this relaxed movement and true delivery to the flow of existence leads me to reflect on how ephemeral and at the same time eternal we are.

Water wire performance - Letter 22

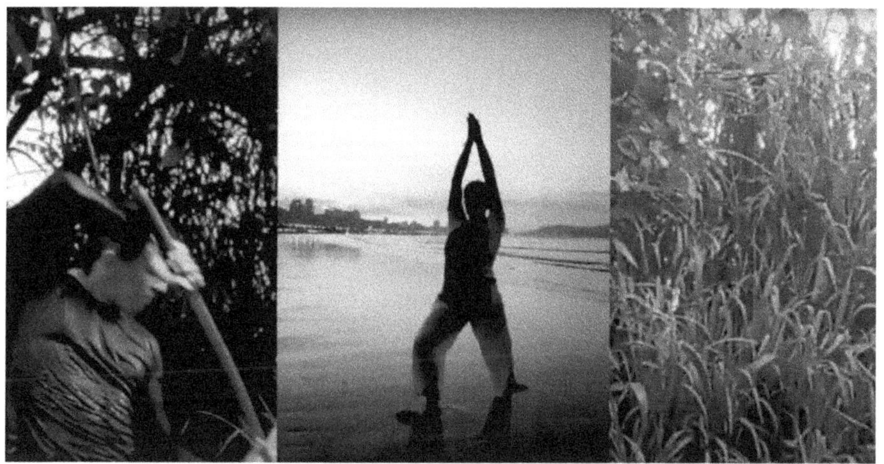

VIDEOPERFORMANCE: https://www.youtube.com/watch?v=F_b73ORsHbs

The yarns of water performance is based on multicultural concepts that dialogue with the present reality in which water on earth is becoming a scarce resource, the approaches of this study are based on authors not only from the field of arts but from other areas that portray our pluriverse reality and that the seas are important for our subsistence (especially in caiçaras and fishermen communities), my method was firstly to observe and explore the environments in a way that could learn more about the local community and their life habits, the tools were raised by the search of empty spaces, the in-between space in which new forms, perceptions and fractions of reality were perceived and translated into the form of movement. The creative process involved explorations of possible movement that could translate into movement the idea that we can be "one" with nature, honoring our roots and ancestry. And the rehearsal system took place with repeated trips to the sea to explore the environment and dialogue with that environment in a gestural way. Also, as i work with music, suggested to my advisor that we put on the kalimba, which is an African instrument and its simple sound is very reminiscent of the sound of drops or streams of water propagating through space. My partner Jonatas, who was also in this video, that his recorded was made in the Garcia neighborhood, in the center of Salvador was very happy in his dialogue under the edge of a sword with a trickle of water, nimbly occupying this space in between.

Rasa Hop- Letter 28

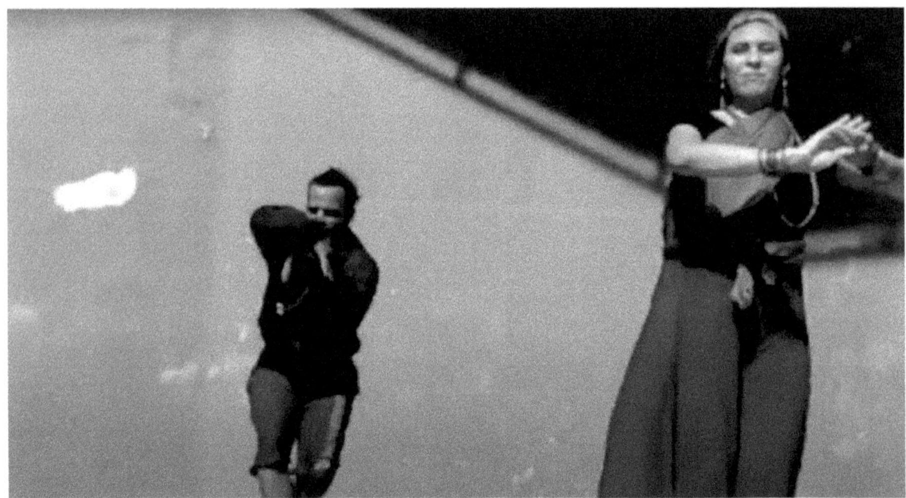

VIDEOPERFORMANCE: https://www.youtube.com/watch?v=7a_XIm9fxzU

RASA HOP: SPINNING ON THEIR OWN FEET

Performance exercises based on the Indian theory of Rasa and the recent discoveries of contemporary science allow the actor-dancer to be a true "athlete of emotions". Rasa is a Sanskrit word that represents juice, essence or flavor and the combination of these flavors: salty, sweet, bitter, acrid and astringent, provide balance in the body's humors. The flavors become an expressive conversation between the universes of dance, theater and music without losing bhava (emotion), truth and sincerity.

Rasa Hop is a work with a circular relationship between the body and emotion, between the inside and the outside, and provides paths for dialogue, construction and creation of emotional scores between body arts, in their different forms of manifestation in the world. Dance is the art of time, and rhythm is based on the aesthetic trait of these expressions.

The Indian Kathak dance, which is the ancient art of storytelling, meets hip hop (based on the contemporary culture of street dances) in crevices, landscapes and passageways of the city of São Paulo in a fluid conversation where the taal meet breaking, and the beatbox chants with the bells (grungos) on the dancer's feet dictate rhythmic beats that allow downrock and a wide range of expressiveness in forms of performance scores that dialogue with each other in complete fusion, with the freeze movements of hip hop and of its dancers, who are also true urban narrators. Indian dance dancers are like storytellers and must train rasas (expressions) and beatbox (singing Indian splints) together with rhythmic percussion in their steps. In this sensory experience where dance assumes its social, anthropological and primitive character, a space is opened for a fertile dialogue in the field of encounter and crossing of cultures and the mind is opened to the game and the flow of creativity. In both languages, the ability to sing and dance what is sung is important for both dancers, creating new rhythmic matrices and emotional scores. Contemporary Indian dance meets hip hop in crevices and cityscapes in a fluid conversation with a wide range of expressiveness in forms of performance scores that dialogue with each other in complete fusion.

RasaHop allows connections and bridges of lived and felt art, thus expanding our soundscape. Art; embodiment; sensoriality; emotions; cognition, performance; ritual; ecstasy; Indian dance; hip hop; shallow-hop; emotional scores; soundscape; ecology of knowledge; intercultural translation; rasa, the art of happiness; body; heart; imagination.

Vídeo: https://youtube.com/watch?v=qoTChrblFQQ&feature=share

Other performances

Performance Durga Rasa Hop:

https://drive.google.com/file/d/1e6a4wkZgxcSTlYIqoWTaQ4cGiZBxk09B/view?usp=drivesdk

Jagat Janani

https://drive.google.com/file/d/16oBpNidvBhdKXpStFcVsVc3RXHJPeyYv/view?usp=drivesdk

Final Considerations

Political art? Maybe so, as long as we accept the potential politics of the transitory, insofar as the change of state of things and the impermanence of life constitute an opportunity to experiment in a space-time of transformation. It is like these anonymous characters who turn to nothing, as if this abstract form that attracts the bodies in front of it (Do they look at her? Do you understand it? To what extent does its existence depend on the facial expression of the person staring at her? And to what extent its meaning, for us, is it related to its apprehension on the part of the witnesses? What do we have in hand? What do we keep before our eyes? Do we reproduce what we see? Do we dramatize, give life, what do we capture? Are we ourselves in what we touch?).

First political lesson: sometime, all the time, the world tells you will turn your back. In it, a voice repeats to us incessantly, mechanically, the same message: "look, I'm here, if only for this moment, in its eternity". Here, the ears are stronger than the eyes. And that voice is all that can be heard.